You Look Beautiful Like That

You Look Beautiful Like That

The Portrait Photographs of Seydou Keïta and Malick Sidibé

Michelle Lamunière

Harvard University Art Museums
Cambridge

Yale University Press
New Haven and London

You Look Beautiful Like That: The Portrait Photographs of Seydou Keïta and Malick Sidibé is the catalogue of an exhibition organized by the Fogg Art Museum, Harvard University Art Museums, Cambridge, Massachusetts, on view 1 September–16 December 2001. The exhibition was funded with the support of the Gurel Student Exhibition Fund.

Distributed by Yale University Press
http://www.yale.edu/yup, ISBN 0-300-09188-5

Library of Congress Cataloging-in-Publication Data

Lamunière, Michelle.
You look beautiful like that : the portrait photographs of Seydou Keïta and Malick Sidibé / Michelle Lamunière.
p. cm.
Catalog of the exhibition held Sept. 1–Dec. 16, 2001 at the Fogg Art Museum.
Includes bibliographical references.
ISBN 1-891771-20-5 (alk. paper)
1. Portrait photography—Mali—Exhibitions.
2. Commercial photography—Mali—Exhibitions.
3. Keïta, Seydou, 1923—Exhibitions.
4. Sidibé, Malick, 1936—Exhibitions. I. Keïta, Seydou, 1923- II. Sidibé, Malick, 1936- III. Fogg Art Museum. IV. Title.

TR680.L314 2001
779'.2'096623—dc21 2001039352

Illustration credits

Figs. 1–6, 8–10, 13, 15–16: All rights reserved, The Metropolitan Museum of Art.
Figs. 7 and 14: Courtesy of Eliot Elisofon Photographic Archives, National Museum of African Art, Smithsonian Institution.
Fig. 11: © Photographer Mountaga Dembélé, courtesy of *Revue Noire*.
Fig. 12: © Malick Sidibé, courtesy of the Contemporary African Art Collection—The Pigozzi Collection, Geneva.
Fig. 17: Photographs © Seydou Keïta, courtesy of *Harper's Bazaar.*
Fig. 18: Photographs © Malick Sidibé, courtesy of *Double, nouveau feminin.*
Page 45: Photograph © Françoise Huguier.
Page 51: Photograph © Baba Maiga.

Catalogue nos. 15–72 courtesy of the Contemporary African Art Collection—The Pigozzi Collection, Geneva.
Catalogue nos. 29–33, 40, 42, 44, 46–48, 50, 53, 57, 60–62, 66, 68, 70, 71 © Seydou Keïta.
Catalogue nos. 15–28, 34–39, 41, 43, 45, 49, 51, 52, 54–56, 58, 59, 63–65, 67, 69, 72 © Malick Sidibé.

Produced by the Publications Department, Harvard University Art Museums
Evelyn Rosenthal, Head of Publications
Editor: Marsha Pomerantz
Design: Becky Hunt
Printer: MacDonald & Evans, Braintree, Massachusetts
Printed in the United States

Contents

Director's Foreword

In photography, the relationship between commercial practice and artistic achievement is an especially interesting, and often vexing, one. The two artists represented here, Seydou Keïta and Malick Sidibé, did not think of themselves as artists when they were making portraits. As Michelle Lamunière says in her essay for this catalogue, they felt their role was "to please their customers by making them look good."

And make them look good they did. The intimacy of these portraits is striking, with some sitters self-conscious and others so free of the constraints of convention. When they do "pose" it is with such flagrant presentation of attitude or such charming and sweet innocence that they hardly appear to be posing at all: they seem all there, every bit of them, their bodies, physiognomies, and personalities, all convincingly of their time, place, and individual ambitions.

We are convinced of the truthfulness of these portraits, and are moved by the obvious sense of trust between photographer and sitter. These portraits are of people made comfortable by the photographer. And the photographers' ability to engender such trust in their sitters is an important part of their artistry, no less than their delight in an almost riotous mix of linear patterns (Keïta, so reminiscent of Matisse) and the hip and sometimes humorous straightforwardness of their posing (Sidibé, like Weegee with a touch of August Sander).

These are sophisticated photographers. And we are very pleased to be presenting their work in this exhibition, drawn from the renowned collection of Jean Pigozzi (Harvard Class of 1974). Mr. Pigozzi's trust in our professionalism and our teaching and training mission, as well as his help with the internship that allowed Michelle to develop this project from initial idea to final installation and publication, were crucial to the exhibition. We are deeply grateful to him, just as we are to Deborah Martin Kao, the Fogg Art Museum's Richard L. Menschel Curator of Photography, and Danielle Hanrahan and Evelyn Rosenthal, heads respectively of the Art Museums' Exhibitions and Publications departments, who together helped Michelle make this project the handsome and important one that it is. We gratefully acknowledge, too, the support of the Gurel Student Exhibition Fund.

But our greatest thanks must go to Michelle herself. A Ph.D. candidate in art history at Boston University specializing in the history of photography, Michelle has been a model intern and colleague, tackling a complicated project with intelligence and enthusiasm and producing an important work of scholarship into the bargain.

We are very pleased to have organized this exhibition and to be sharing its artists' and curator's work with a larger audience through the distribution of this catalogue by Yale University Press.

James Cuno
Elizabeth and John Moors Cabot Director

I would like to express my sincerest gratitude to James Cuno, my professor and primary inspiration when I was an undergraduate at Vassar College, for his support over the years and for the opportunity to develop an exhibition and catalogue around such incredible material. I am also beholden to Seydou Keïta and Malick Sidibé for taking the time to talk with me about their careers as photographers and for sharing their experiences of portrait making in Bamako as well as their wonderful photographs.

Harvard alumnus Jean Pigozzi has generously lent the photographs by Keïta and Sidibé in the exhibition from his Contemporary African Art Collection, based in Geneva. I thank André Magnin, curator of this collection, for his assistance during my research trip to Paris. I worked closely with Philippe Boutté on the logistical details of putting the exhibition and catalogue together and am indebted to him for his professionalism and good humor. I also gladly acknowledge Philippe Salaün for creating the modern prints of the photographers' work.

For their assistance in the planning phases and during my visit to Bamako, I am eternally grateful to Ousmane Macina, Caleb Kissling, Mike Sarabia, Mahamadou Yaressi, and, especially, Baba Maiga, whose interest in the project and gift of friendship made my time in Bamako that much more extraordinary.

I am obliged to the following scholars for their careful reading of and crucial comments on early drafts of the catalogue essay: Lauri Firstenberg, a New York-based independent curator; Christraud M. Geary, curator of the Eliot Elisofon Archives at the National Museum of African Art, Smithsonian Institution; Laura U. Marks, a writer and programmer of independent media and associate professor of film studies at Carleton University, Ottawa; Steven Nelson, assistant professor of African and African American Art History at the University of California, Los Angeles; and Kim Sichel, associate professor of art history at Boston University.

I would also like to express my appreciation to Christraud Geary and to Virginia-Lee Webb, associate research curator in the Department of the Arts of Africa, Oceania, and the Americas at the Metropolitan Museum of Art, for their assistance and for generously lending historical images of Africa from their collections.

Lia Brozgal, a graduate student in Harvard's Department of Romance Languages, transcribed and translated the artists' interviews. I am grateful for her skill in conveying the photographers' voices in her translations. My fellow interns at the Harvard University Art Museums, Catherine Blais, Tanja Maka, and Darius Spieth, also gave generously of their time to assist with other aspects of language translation.

I would like to thank Michael C. Vazquez, Trevor Corson, and Richard Swartz of *Transition* magazine for sharing my enthusiasm about these photographs and for publishing excerpts of my interview with Sidibé.

For their expert assistance in the mounting of the exhibition, I am particularly indebted to Danielle Hanrahan and her capable staff in Exhibitions; Craigen Bowen in the Straus Center for Conservation; and assistant registrar Amanda Prugh. A very special thanks to Becky Hunt, Marsha Pomerantz, and Evelyn Rosenthal of the Publications Department for their editorial skill and creativity in the production of this catalogue. I would also like to acknowledge my colleagues in the Agnes B. Mongan Center, especially Michael Dumas, who assisted with many details of this project.

For their friendship and encouragement through all phases of this project, as well as life, I'd like to recognize Jülide Aker, Karen Haas, Jaimey Hamilton, Stacey McCarroll, Christine Tan, Jenna Webster, and my family.

Finally, thanks from the bottom of my heart to the Fogg's curator of photography, Deborah Martin Kao, my friend and mentor, for her guidance, support, and thoughtful comments throughout the production of the catalogue and exhibition, and for challenging me to take the project to higher and higher levels of quality and achievement.

This catalogue is dedicated to my mother, Janice, for her boundless love and support and for her never-ending belief in my abilities.

You Look Beautiful Like That:
The Portrait Photographs of Seydou Keïta and Malick Sidibé

Michelle Lamunière

During the decades before and after Mali's independence from France in 1960, Seydou Keïta and Malick Sidibé operated highly regarded commercial photography studios in the capital city of Bamako. They were among the most interesting and active photographers in the city, catering to a burgeoning middle class and making tens of thousands of portraits for members of their communities. Although each of the photographers had a unique vision, their work can be seen as representative of the development of studio portraiture in mid-twentieth-century West Africa and the ways in which African photographers both maintained and expanded earlier traditions. To their clients, sitting for a portrait and then displaying it at home or sending it to family and friends was a potent means of self-definition at a time of considerable social change. It is important to remember that, although they felt their work was beautiful, Keïta and Sidibé did not consider themselves artists at the time they were making portraits. As commercial photographers, their role was to please their customers by making them look good.

Since the early 1990s they have gained increasing recognition outside of Africa for, among other qualities, the formal strength of their photographs. Keïta's portraits were first brought to the attention of the art world in the 1991 exhibition *Africa Explores* at the Center for African Art in New York. Sidibé is best known for his lively images of Bamako youth at private parties and Sunday picnics on the banks of the Niger River, which were first seen in the West in 1995 at the Fondation Cartier pour l'Art Contemporain in Paris.

Presented as large exhibition prints, the portraits of Keïta and Sidibé are graphically stunning and psychologically engaging. Decorative textiles and vivid, clashing patterns; elaborate adornment; a mixture of traditional and contemporary dress; and prominently displayed consumer goods appear in symmetrical compositions featuring constructed poses and high contrast. The images seem to reflect a combination of self-consciousness and pride of presentation in the subjects. For a deeper appreciation of these images, however, it is important to understand that this reissue of work from the 1940s through 1980s for predominantly Western audiences, although sanctioned by the artists,[1] constitutes a dramatic recasting of its form and function. In their original context, Keïta's and Sidibé's portrait photographs were privately commissioned and printed at an intimate scale;[2] here, in prints ranging from 42 x 35 to 77 x 60 centimeters, the subjects are anonymous and it is the photographs' presentation as works of art that speaks to viewers. To convey a sense of the original intimacy of the images, some commercial prints by Sidibé are included in this exhibition (cat. nos. 15–28). Regrettably, few prints by

Keïta have survived outside the context of their creation.

Writing about what is lost when photographs that once served a utilitarian function are converted into "art," the critic Martha Rosler observed, "the denial that the meaning of photographs rests in their rootedness in the stream of life preserves the photography at the level of object, a mere item of value hanging on a wall."[3] Displayed as they are here, Keïta's and Sidibé's photographs have far more than commodity value. The nature of their appeal has been the subject of a number of essays, articles, and interviews published in the West. André Magnin, curator of the Geneva-based Contemporary African Art Collection, brought both photographers to the attention of the West and edited a major volume of photographs by each of them. Art historian Elizabeth Bigham has analyzed the authorial role of both the photographer and the subject in Keïta's photographs. Writer and curator Robert Storr has remarked that it is the tension between what Keita's sitters brought to the portrait session and the pictorial framework devised by the photographer that attracts the viewer's eye. Scholar and filmmaker Manthia Diawara has discussed Keita's photographs in the context of what he calls the "the myth of Bamako," the city at the birth of modernity in West Africa, and Sidibé's work as it reflects Bamako youths' embrace of rock and roll, rebellion against authority, and a black "diaspora aesthetic" in their clothing and consumer habits.[4]

Building on these earlier interpretations, the exhibition *You Look Beautiful Like That* explores Keïta's and Sidibé's remarkable work with an emphasis on its place in the context of portrait photography in West Africa, and particularly the use of portraits by African photographers and subjects as a site of self-definition. It demonstrates the work's rootedness in the history and society of Mali while acknowledging the necessarily different form and context in which the images are viewed on the walls of a museum.

Commercial portrait photography first came to Mali in the 1930s, as it did to much of the French West African interior. Keïta (born c. 1921) was one of the first African photographers to work in Bamako, beginning in the 1940s. Although clearly connected to long-established conventions of studio portraiture, his mesmerizing portraits convey a unique expressive style that both confirms his clients' status within the community and reflects their desire to be seen as cosmopolitan. Sidibé (born c. 1935) adapted that expressive style for a new generation. As portrait conventions and societal roles became more flexible in the 1960s and 1970s, the subjects of his photographs took a more active, often theatrical, role in constructing their self-images. Although the names and professions of many of the sitters have been lost, their identities, aspirations, and fantasies are communicated through clothing, accessories, props, and poses. In contrast to the photographs produced by Western observers, the portraits of Keïta and Sidibé are the result of African photographers controlling the camera to create images of African subjects for an African audience.

From its introduction into Africa in the 1840s, the camera had largely been deployed by Europeans: commercial photographers used it to fulfill the voyeuristic yearnings of armchair adventurers back home, missionaries to document their work in "saving" native peoples from their presumed savagery, anthropologists and ethnographers for the "objective" study of African societies and cultures, and colonial powers to justify their presence in Africa. Photography was therefore instrumental in affirming visual codes and stereotypes through which the West interpreted Africa and its people.[5] Postcards, widely distributed in Africa and Europe in the late nineteenth and early twentieth centuries, helped disseminate these stereotypes. Even for Western audiences today, "Africa" often conjures up the *National Geographic* model of the noble savage, or images of famine and ethnic strife. In contrast, Keïta and Sidibé collaborated with their subjects to produce images that had significance within their own society. In Bambara, the language widely spoken in Mali, there is an expression *i ka nyè tan*, which means "you look beautiful like that."[6] Keïta and Sidibé's portraits flatter the sitters, presenting them in the best possible light.

In their original context, Keïta's and Sidibé's portrait photographs exist at the threshold between private and public life. They are most fundamentally mementos of people, souvenirs of special moments and events. Small-scale prints were exchanged as tangible proof of friendship and love. Photographs were put in albums, tacked on walls, or framed. As Malians migrated to the cities from rural areas, they mailed portrait photographs back home. Keïta recalls that clients would specifically request the postcard format so they could send the photograph in a letter.[7]

But photographic portraits were also symbols of wealth and social importance, achieving iconic status, especially during Keïta's time. Framed photographs of family members and community leaders were prominently displayed in parlors and at important gatherings to acknowledge respect for and involvement with the subjects and present them as models of comportment (see fig. 12). Often the number and size of photographs displayed was a gauge of affluence. And the fact that images privately commissioned for domestic settings were often shared with the larger community conferred special status on photographers as creators and guardians of visual memory.

In previously published interviews Sidibé and Keïta both spoke of the long lines of people who used to wait in front of their studios on Saturdays and around Muslim holidays when, as Sidibé described it, "People saved up and bought brand new clothes for the festival. They made the most of it and had themselves photographed in their new clothes."[8] At times the crowds around the studios were so thick that customers couldn't get through. "Africans love photography," Sidibé said. It is "the very emblem of the self. People want to preserve themselves, their faces ... the person knows that he can look in the mirror and see his own face ... what a discovery! The camera functions like a mirror. It proves one's existence, or at least a part of one's existence. It leaves you with a permanent trace."[9]

In spite of the excitement generated by photography, many of Keïta's and Sidibé's images capture the restrained facial expressions and heightened degree of composure that were a response to the formality of the portrait sitting and, early on, its novelty. As Keïta noted, "To have your photo taken was an important event. The person had to be made to look his or her best. Often they became serious, and I think they were also intimidated by the camera. It was a new sensation for them."[10] By the time Sidibé opened his studio in 1962, however, portrait photographs in Bamako had become ubiquitous, and there was more experimentation with informal poses and individual expressions, as well as role playing.

Photography in West Africa

Itinerant European and American photographers traveling the trade route to India and Australia around the Cape of Good Hope established portrait studios in west coast port cities as early as 1845.[11] By the 1860s African photographers with both European and African clienteles were operating permanent studios or working as itinerant photographers in coastal towns and trade centers. While the coastal towns were opened early to Western influence, the inland regions remained relatively isolated until the 1880s.[12]

Even though photography originated in the West, its reception and production in Africa was structured by African cultural values. The earliest photographers were part of an elite, often racially mixed, society that adopted colonial forms, including portraiture, and adapted them to their own needs. Both studio and itinerant photographers appropriated the conventions of studio photography, including compositional centrality, full-length figures shown frontally, shallow pictorial space, and the incorporation of backdrops and accessories. It is difficult to distinguish between the photographs made by Europeans and those made by Africans in these beginning years; one way to track the development of West African studio photography in its earliest phases is through postcards.

Representations of Africans were widely distributed on postcards from the 1890s well into the 1930s. The cards functioned as records of local events and personalities as well as colonial propaganda and documents of "primitive" cultures. They were purchased by tourists and colonial residents, but infrequently by Africans themselves. The estimated number of different views produced in colonial West Africa was 7,210 from about 1900 to 1918, 930 between 1919 and 1939, and 600 from 1945 to 1963.[13] The French, German, and Belgian postcard industries were particularly strong, although there were also important African producers.

One of the biggest European producers of postcards was François-Edmond Fortier, based in Dakar, Senegal. Born in France in 1862, Fortier had moved to Africa by 1899. His business operated until the 1920s, catering to French colonials, traders, and administrators and other Europeans who lived in or traveled through Senegal. He had a stock of at least 4,000 postcard images that he reissued during his lifetime (he stopped photographing in 1910), including scenes of colonial and native life and points of interest throughout

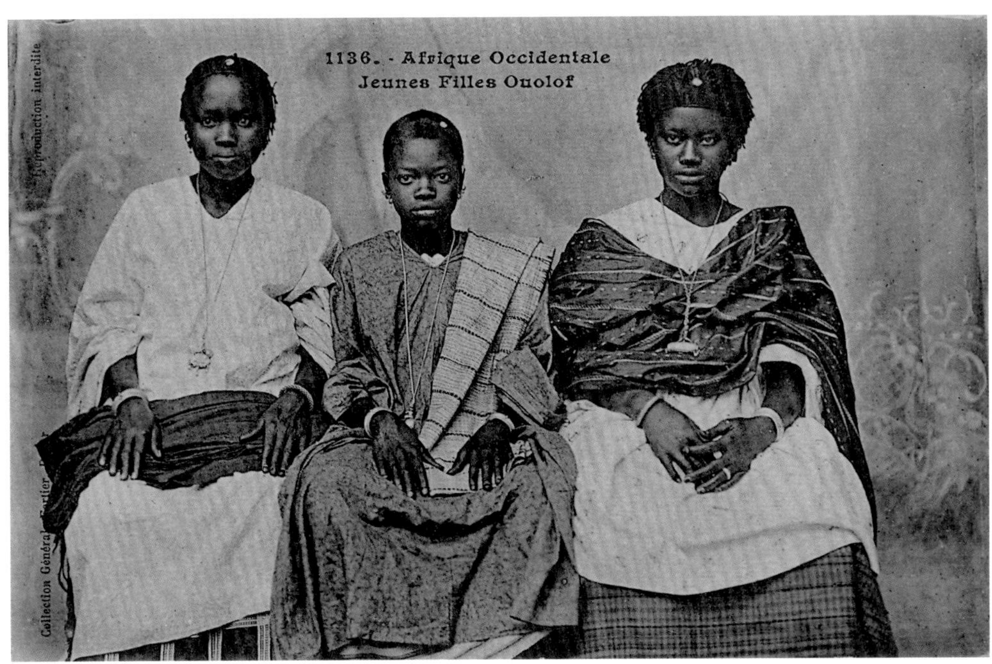

Fig. 1. François-Edmond Fortier, *1136. Afrique Occidentale, Jeunes Filles Ouolof* [West Africa, Young Wolof Girls], c. 1900–10. Postcard (cat. no. 1).

West Africa. On a trip to Mali in 1905–6, Fortier photographed Bamako's post office and train station, the mosque and market in Ségou, a butcher's shop and the arrival of a caravan transporting salt in Timbuktu. Fortier also took formulaic photographs of African people, especially of seductively posed women. Many of his postcards, including a view of three African women sitting before a decorative, painted backdrop and captioned *Afrique Occidentale, Jeunes Filles Ouolof,* are reflective of images produced by European studios (fig. 1).

Like their European counterparts, early African photographers created images for the tourist trade in addition to operating portrait studios. Alphonso Lisk-Carew, a Creole living in Freetown, Sierra Leone, established a business in 1905 and was joined by his brother Arthur in 1918. Freetown was a city in which many residents persisted in African social and religious practices privately, but in public, with encouragement from the Western administration and missionaries, adopted European customs, including the Victorian pastime of photography.[14]

Lisk-Carew took portraits of local and British clienteles and official pictures for the colonial administration. The studio was also well known for its extensive stock of postcards, which were sold up and down the west coast of Africa well into the 1950s. Working with glass negatives and daylight, Lisk-Carew photographed both urban and rural street scenes,

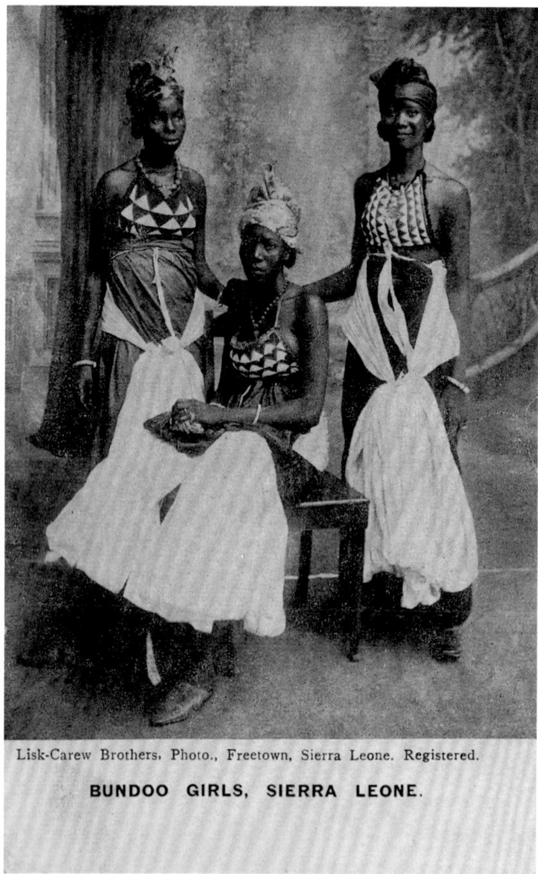

Fig. 2. Lisk-Carew Brothers, *Bundoo Girls, Sierra Leone,* c. 1910. Postcard, halftone (cat. no. 2).

landscapes, and African women in various states of undress. The composition and backdrop of the Lisk-Carew postcard *Bundoo Girls* exemplify his use of long-established conventions of studio portraiture (fig. 2). Three African girls, two standing and one seated, are posed in front of an elaborate painted scene of classical ruins. Like Fortier, Lisk-Carew was catering to the desires of a predominantly colonial market.

A postcard image by a photographer named Khalilou, who worked in Libreville, Gabon, is an example of the African adaptation of European conventions: a group of women poses in front of a backdrop; the classical architecture depicted contrasts with the patterned textiles of their dress and the fabric apparently thrown hastily on the ground in front of them (fig. 3). The photographer betrays the constructed environment of the studio by revealing an exterior setting that includes trees and hanging laundry, occupying about a third of the image on the right side. Although Khalilou posed the subjects, the grouping of four seated women with a fifth standing to the right does not reflect the emphasis on structured, symmetrical compositions normally associated with studio portraiture.

Exploring postcard production in Africa to determine whether African and European photographers exercised different visions, historian and curator Christraud Geary identifies as crucial issues the sitter's intention, the interaction between photographer and subject in the construction of the image, and, most important, the distinction between public and private images.[15] As the examples of these postcards suggest, some card photographs by both European and African studios likely represent private portrait commissions that subsequently were captioned for the tourist trade as "ethnographic" representations.

The image of a man wearing a traditional African boubou and holding an umbrella and a cigarette on a postcard by A. Albaret entitled *Guinée Française—Conakry—Type Soussons [sic]* clearly represents a private portrait (fig. 4). Another example is *Conakry—Famille Soussou,* by an unknown photographer (fig. 5). In the first image, a man gazes confidently off to the left, smiling slightly, as if in pleased anticipation of the resulting portrait. Geary describes this conversion of individual into generic subject as an example of the subject stepping out of the private realm and into the public domain.[16] Unlike the portraits of Keïta and Sidibé, which remained in the private realm of family, friends, and community, the postcard portraits and their accompanying captions depersonalize their subjects, transforming them into anonymous types.[17]

Other images from the early twentieth century suggest that sitters were invited to the studio to have their portraits taken with the intention of distributing them as postcards. This may be the case with *The Young Native Girl* by F. Arkhurst, an African photographer from Côte d'Ivoire (fig. 6). A young African girl, exposed from the waist up, wears a wrap, necklace, and headscarf. She is seated beside a table covered with African textiles on which a vase of flowers rests. The painted backdrop depicts a European-style salon or parlor. Like the "classical" backdrops in other postcards, it creates a disquieting juxtaposition of African subject and European setting. The visual disjunction apparent in such images might have been intended to emphasize the civilizing of "primitive" peoples, as did early postcards of Africans using the equipment of modern life, such as *Négresses modernisées* from the Belgian Congo, which depicts two African women posing with a bicycle (fig. 7). This combination of traditionally African and Western objects also appears in the portraits of Keïta

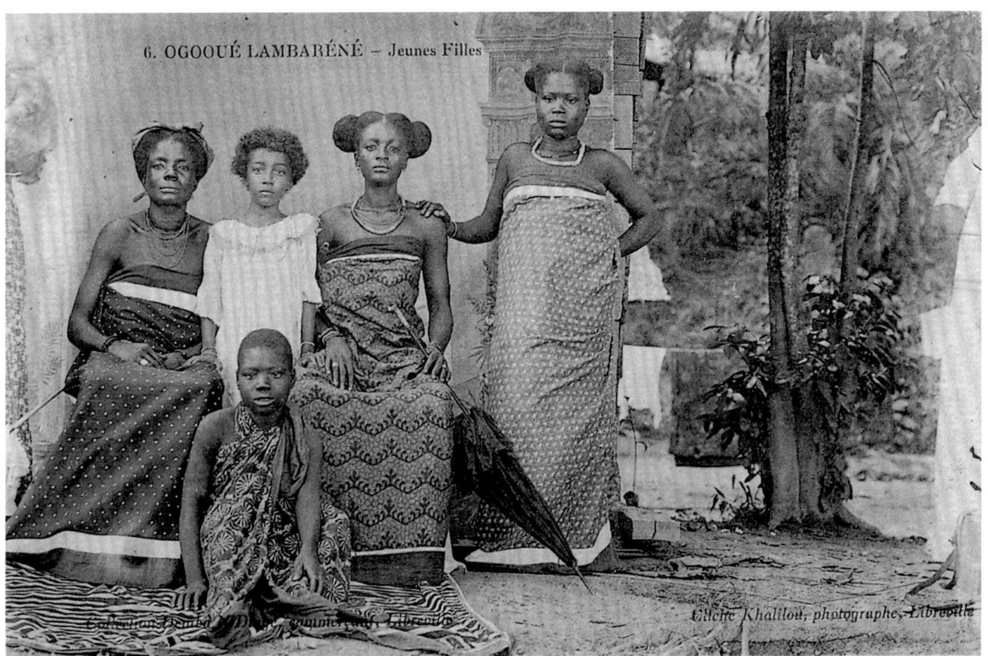

Fig. 3. Khalilou, *6. Ogooué Lambaréné—Jeunes Filles* [Ogooué Lambaréné—Young Girls], c. 1900–15. Postcard (cat. no. 3).

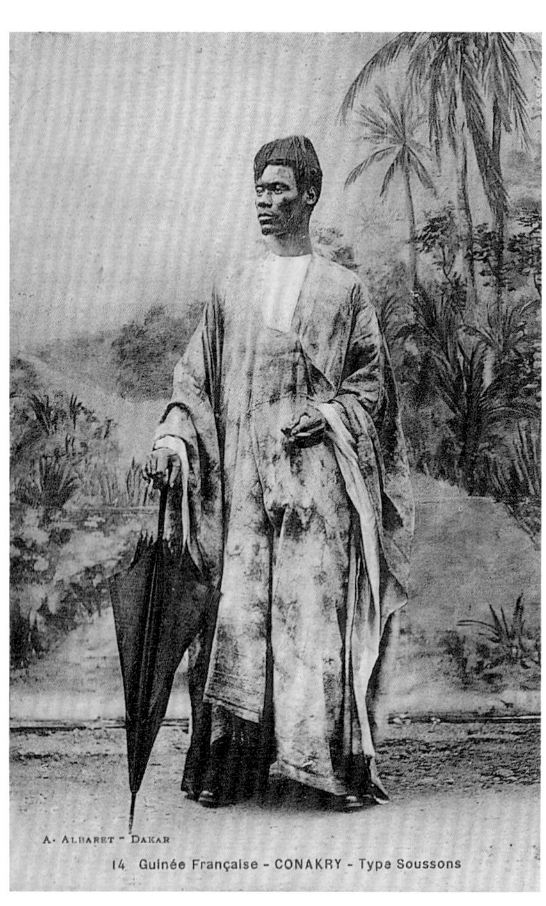

Fig. 4. Photographer unknown, *14. Guinée Française—Conakry—Type Soussons [sic]* [French Guinea—Conakry—Soussons *(sic)* Type], c. 1900–15. Postcard (cat. no. 4).

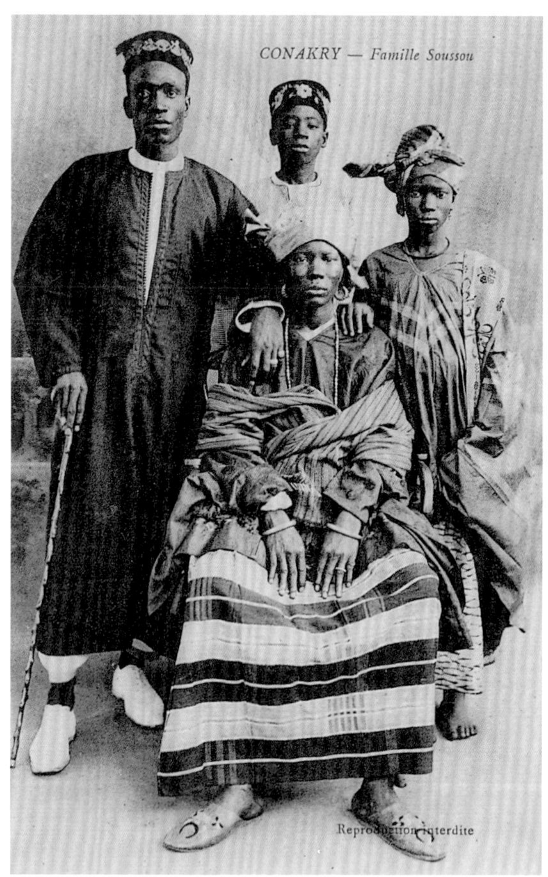

Fig. 5. Photographer unknown, *Conakry—Famille Soussou* [Conakry—Soussou Family], c. 1900–15. Postcard (cat. no. 5).

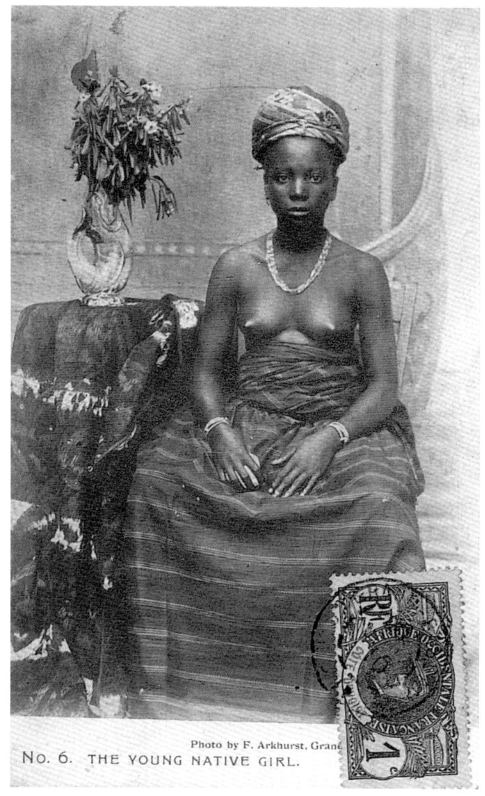

Fig. 6. F. Arkhurst, *No. 6 The Young Native Girl*, c. 1900–15. Postcard, lithograph (cat. no. 6).

and Sidibé, but there it was the clients' choice to have themselves photographed with objects identified with the West as a means of expressing their urbanity and enthusiasm for modern life.

Two private portraits of Africans from the early twentieth century by an unidentified photographer, probably from Côte d'Ivoire, show the appropriation of aesthetic conventions popular with both colonial and African clienteles. They also provide compelling examples of the range of self-representation by African subjects. In one photograph, an African couple poses in front of a backdrop painted to depict a mystical landscape (fig. 8). The woman is dressed in African style; the man, in a European suit, keeps one hand in his pocket, pulling his jacket aside in typical Western fashion to reveal a vest and watch fob. The emphasis is on a balanced composition, composed figures, shallow pictorial space, and a backdrop that offers a sense of location. Nearly every aspect of this photograph evokes a European studio portrait. The most obvious exception is the African textile, which is draped in front of the backdrop. The painted backdrop transports the sitters into a classical landscape, but the textile grounds them in Africa.

In contrast, the other image by the same photographer shows a seated couple wearing

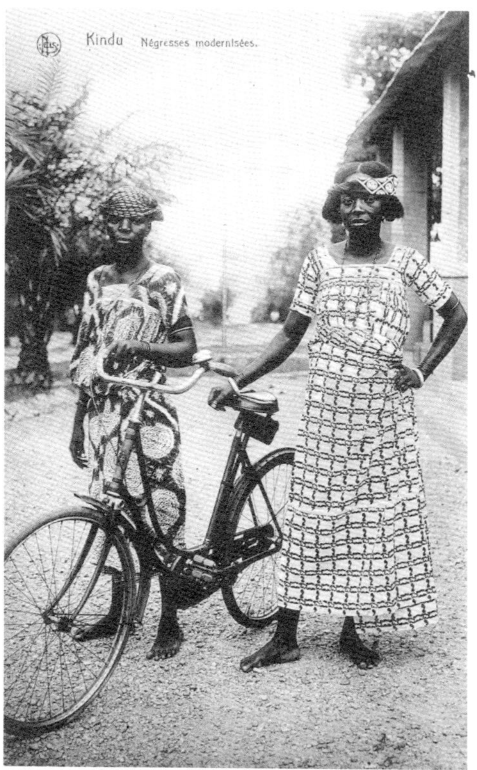

Fig. 7. Photographer unknown, Kindu, Belgian Congo, *Kindu—Négresses modernisées* [Kindu—Modernized black women], c. 1915. Postcard, collotype (cat. no. 7).

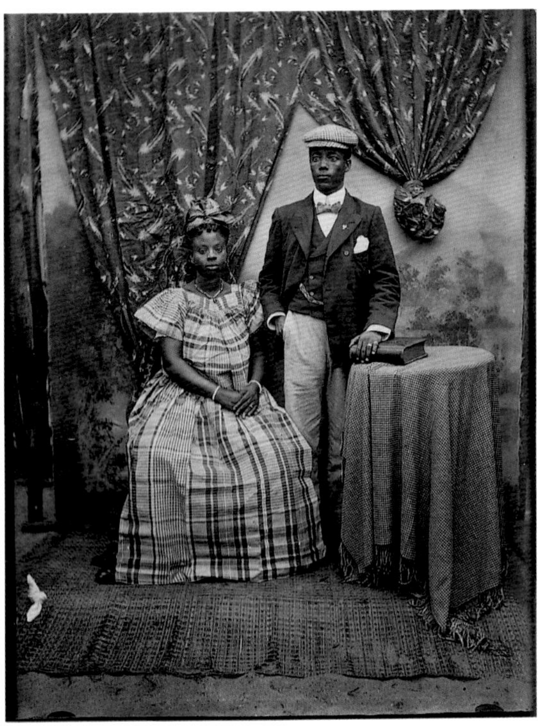

Fig. 8. Photographer unknown, possibly Côte d'Ivoire, *Untitled* (exterior studio portrait), c. 1900–50. Gelatin silver print (cat. no. 13).

primarily African clothing and adornments, including a headscarf, rings, and necklaces (fig. 9). In this case, the textile completely covers the backdrop. Western influence is indicated by the umbrella leaning against the man's right knee, his hat, and the pipe he's "smoking." Though this couple wear distinctly African dress, the accessories suggest their desire to be associated with conveniences and luxuries introduced by the colonialists.

The outdoor setting and African subjects support the idea that the maker of these portraits was an itinerant African photographer, or at least one without a permanent studio. In rural areas portrait photography was the exclusive profession of Africans, although few prints and little documentation remain. In both images there is a worn woven mat on what appears to be sand or dirt in the foreground. In the first image, the backdrop is suspended from thin logs rather than a prefabricated structure or frame, indicating that it was improvised. The backdrop is out of focus in several areas, probably displaced by a breeze. The photographer likely offered his clients a choice of backdrops and props, and the prints raise fascinating questions about what these cross-cultural options meant to the sitters and the self-images they wanted to project.

African photographers working in coastal cities with both European and African clients—the latter of an elite class that participated in colonial society—tended to follow the conventions of photographic portraiture during these early years. It was the itinerant photographers traveling to rural areas outside of colonial influence who were instrumental in developing a unique African style of photographic portraiture.

Initially, commissioning a portrait was a luxury that few Africans outside the city elite could afford. However, in the 1930s demand began to come from all classes, including the poorest members of urban and rural society. According to one historian, there was little need for photography until identity cards were required by the colonial authorities conducting population censuses and tracing migration from rural to urban areas and from country to country.[18] Although formal portraits were significantly different, the need for identity photographs meant broader access to photographic technology in rural areas and may have spurred an interest in photography as a vehicle for self-definition.

While photography spread quickly along the coast and within British colonies such as Sierra Leone, it was rarely practiced by African photographers in the French-dominated interior before the 1930s. Until then, photographic images were seen almost exclusively through postcards, such as the image of a Wolof merchant's family taken in Nioro (fig. 10); in the early part of the twentieth century there were about fifteen postcard publishers in Mali.[19] Both distance from the coastal cities and the repression of French colonial regimes were likely reasons for the delay in the spread of photography to the interior.[20] British colonial policy was one of "indirect rule," which encouraged the training of local workers, including photographers, to assist the colonial and commercial administrations.[21] In the French colonies, however, the production and circulation of images by African photographers were controlled. Authorities were likely concerned that Africans would use the camera to more accurately record the lives and cultures of African peoples, destroying the illusion of exoticism or exposing French policies of forced labor that contradicted the celebratory view of colonialism perpetuated in postcards.

The path of commercial portrait photography in the urban areas of the West African interior can be traced by looking at its practice in Bamako. France colonized what is now Mali, creating French Sudan, in 1898. Located on the Niger River where traders from the West met caravans from the Sahara, Bamako had been an important trading center before French domination. After a railroad line from Saint-Louis, Senegal, to Bamako was completed in 1904 and the colonial administration relocated to Bamako in 1908, the city's status was secured. The post–World War II period was one of rapid urbanization and development, with workers streaming into Bamako from surrounding regions. By the late 1940s, when Keïta opened his studio, Bamako had become an important urban center.[22] The population in the city continued to grow, rising from 37,000 in 1945 to 129,000 in 1960.[23]

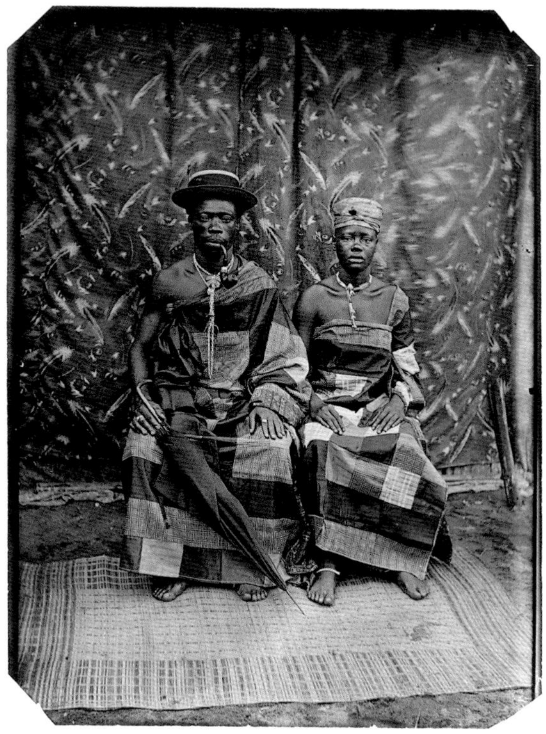

Fig. 9. Photographer unknown, possibly Côte d'Ivoire, *Untitled* (exterior studio portrait), c. 1900–50. Gelatin silver print (cat. no. 14).

The city's first photo shop, Photo-Hall Soudanais, was opened in 1935 by a Frenchman, Pierre Garnier, who spoke Bambara fluently. Although he was not Bamako's first photographer, he is often cited as such.[24] After 1940 he hired Sudanese employees, who did developing and printing, made enlargements, and ran the bookshop. Because there was little competition within the interior, Photo-Hall Soudanais serviced much of inland French West Africa and had clients as far away as Côte d'Ivoire, Dahomey (now Benin), and Togo. Garnier also sold equipment and made photographs for identity cards, portraits, and postcards that were well known throughout French Sudan. Among his customers were members of the first generation of Malian photographers, including Mountaga Dembélé and Seydou Keïta.

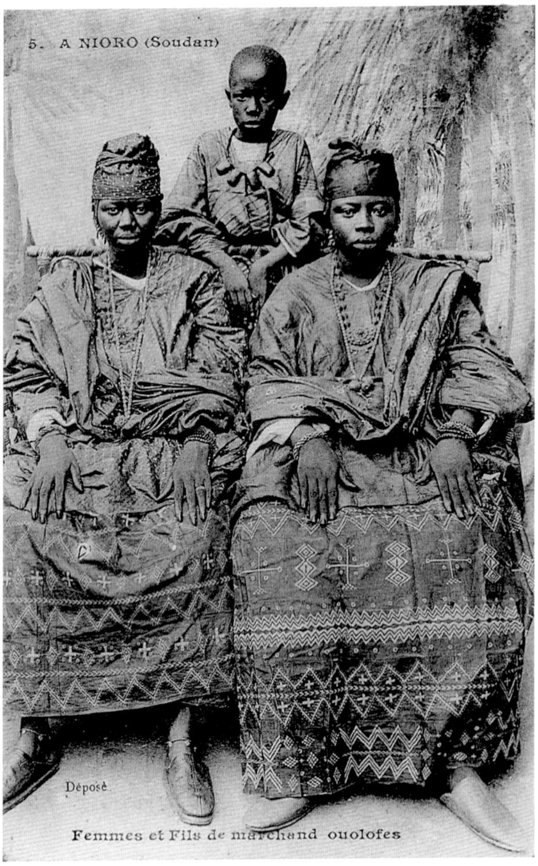

5. A NIORO (Soudan)

Déposé

Femmes et Fils de marchand ouolofes

Fig. 10. Photographer unknown, *5. A Nioro (Soudan). Femmes et Fils de marchand ouolofes* [At Nioro (Sudan), Wives and Son of Wolof Merchant], c. 1900–15. Postcard (cat. no. 8).

Most portrait studios run by African photographers in the West African interior were opened after 1945. Some of the photographers had learned their craft while serving in the French army during World War II. Others, such as Sidibé, were assistants in studios owned by Europeans before setting up their own businesses; still others worked as itinerants. "It wasn't the love of the camera that first drew Africans to photography, it was the promise of financial gain and respectable employment," Sidibé has remarked. "Once we had the hang of it, [however,] ... that first taste turned into a genuine hunger, and a real passion for the art of photography was born."[25]

The first Malian photographer to establish a studio in Bamako was Mountaga Dembélé, also known as Mountaga Kouyâté. Unfortunately, little of his work has survived. Born in 1919, Dembélé began photographing in 1935. In 1945 he returned from military service in Europe and resumed his job as a primary-school teacher, working throughout French Sudan. When he was not teaching, he continued his photographic work. A portrait by Dembélé from c. 1940 depicting a young mother and her baby provides a representative example of his work (fig. 11). The woman, in a dark patterned dress and headdress, is seated in profile with her head turned toward the camera. Her child, in a light-colored dress and bonnet, gazes off to the left while resting quietly in the mother's lap. Behind them is a patterned textile with a leaf-and-flower motif. The lights and darks of the backdrop contrast and combine with those of the sitters' clothing to create a striking decorative effect.

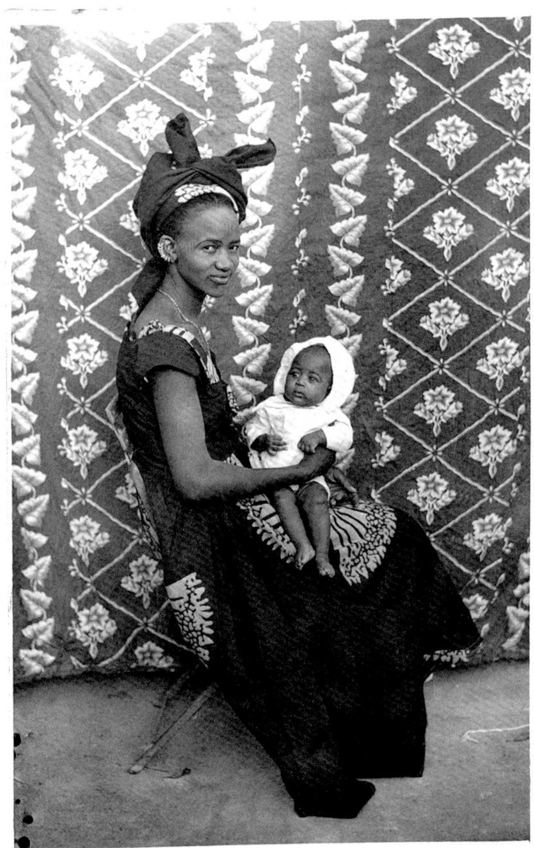

Fig. 11. Mountaga Dembélé, *Untitled*, Bamako, c. 1940. Gelatin silver print, 15 x 10 cm.

Dembélé's portrait exemplifies how the tradition and aesthetic of photographic portraiture evolved from the first African photographers, such as Lisk-Carew, who created portraits for a Creole community that embraced aspects of both African and colonial society. As the private portraits from Côte d'Ivoire show, African photographers working outside of urban areas began to incorporate elements, such as textile backdrops, that appealed specifically to African customers. Like the anonymous maker of those images, Dembélé was not obligated to work for both African and colonial societies, and therefore was freer to modify portrait conventions to create a new aesthetic. A comparison of Dembélé's work with photographs by Keïta reveals a direct lineage of modified portrait conventions, including poses and the use of a patterned backdrop.

Born in Bamako, Seydou Keïta spent the early years of his life apprenticing with his father as a furniture-maker. It was in the 1930s, as Bamako grew into a modern city, that Keïta began to experiment with photography. His uncle, Tièmòkò, had recently returned from Senegal with a 6 x 9 Kodak Brownie camera, which he gave to Keïta along with eight frames of film.[26] Keïta has said that the figures in these very first photographs looked like "skeletons," meaning that the images were unsuccessful, because his subjects, and sometimes he himself, moved while the picture was being taken. He also confesses that he did not know that the camera had three speeds that needed to be adjusted to accommodate different light levels.[27] He started by taking pictures of his family and the apprentices in his father's workshop. Eventually people seeing him with a camera would ask him for portraits—some of which he did in the street and some at the subjects' homes. Although he continued to work as a carpenter, Keïta began photographing professionally in 1939.[28] Around 1945, he bought a 6 x 9 box camera with glass plates, and later, a used 9 x 12 camera.

Keïta says that he had no official training in photography and was not exposed to any Western publications or photographic work in Bamako. However, early in his career he worked closely with both Pierre Garnier and Mountaga Dembélé. Keïta likely absorbed the conventions of studio portraiture through postcard images as well. Dembélé has stated that Keïta understood the mystique of photography early on and quickly assimilated the techniques that he taught him, such as the effective posing of sitters.[29] Garnier gave him basic tips, such as keeping his hands still while shooting, and sold him materials, showing him how they were used.[30] Dembélé taught Keïta the developing process and gave him the use of his darkroom, where Keïta began printing both his and Dembélé's photographs in 1948.[31] Around the same time Keïta bought a 13 x 18 box camera from Garnier. The shutter had been destroyed, so in order to take a photograph, once he had set up the shot, he removed the lens cap to expose the film. Keïta recounts that at first he spoiled many pictures, but through trial and error, learned how to read light levels to determine the correct exposure time.[32] All his photographs after 1949 were taken in this manner.[33]

In 1948 Keïta opened his own studio in a lively part of the city, Bamako-Koura (New Bamako), where he continues to live today. Bamako-Koura was close to the train station that linked Bamako with Dakar and was thus a point of contact with outside influences. It was also the site of the post office, the zoo, the Soudan Club, and the Soudan Ciné, a movie theater where the characters in B- and C-grade movies became the inspiration for the tough-guy poses seen in many of Keïta's portraits. The most frequented spot was the city's bustling market, the Marché Rose.

Because his shop was located in this animated neighborhood, Keïta had an advantage over other photographers. His clients were members of Bamako's elite class, including office clerks, shopkeepers, employees of the colonial government, and politicians. Even Modibo Keita, the leader of Mali's new government after independence and a relative of Keïta's, came for sittings before he became president. In addition, people from Upper Volta (now Burkina Faso), Côte d'Ivoire, Senegal, and Niger would stop by Keïta's studio if they were passing through Bamako. Knowledge of his work spread by word of mouth: "There were a lot of curious people who wanted to see how I worked and who had never seen a camera before."[34] Two former apprentices from his days as a carpenter also took samples of his work to the train station to drum up business.[35]

Keïta's portrait sittings often took as long as an hour, and for each exposure he always made a minimum of three prints. He never made more than two photographs per portrait—if people moved, Keïta told them it was their fault that the picture didn't come out.[36] At first he photographed in his courtyard by daylight, but once established, he purchased three lamps of five hundred watts each so that he could make portraits at night.[37] He preferred natural light, but many of his customers desired prints with the lighter skin tones produced by artificial light. Those images were more expensive because of the added cost of electricity.[38]

Keïta made tens of thousands of portraits in the course of his career. He didn't usually know his customers personally, not even their names, so he has archived his negatives according to pose, such as single full-length figures, single half-length figures, couples, and groups, which are then subdivided by date and gender. Keïta stamped his portraits PHOTO KEÏTA SEYDOU to identify himself as the creator. When he began his business the prices were 25 CFAF (Communauté Financière Africaine francs) for a 6 x 9 print, 100 for a 9 x 12, and 150 for a 13 x 18. His preferred format was 13 x 18 because he could make a contact print from the negative of the same size.[39] The few enlargements requested by clients were processed by Pierre Garnier's studio.

In 1962 Keïta became the official photographer of Mali's newly independent government, documenting events such as official visits and meetings of heads of state. He did not want to close his studio, but the government job offered prestige, and was represented to him as his patriotic duty. Although at first officials indicated that he could continue his portrait work, in 1963 or 1964 he was pressured to close his business because the administration did not want him working outside an official capacity. According to Keïta, his photographs from this period are government property and therefore inaccessible. His studio was cared for by family members until his retirement in 1977, but in the same year, all his cameras and tripods were stolen, which temporarily curtailed his photographic practice.

During the decades before and after Malian independence, Bamako continued to undergo dramatic population growth and economic expansion. New buildings included colleges and hospitals, and in 1957 the first bridge over the Niger River was completed. Portrait photography became a popular phenomenon, and there were new photo studios, such as La Croix du Sud and Photo Service, where Sidibé got his start. The second generation of Malian photographers came of age during this time. Many learned photography through apprenticeships with members of the earlier generation, such as Keïta. Along with darkroom procedures they absorbed conventions of posing and studio setup that had evolved into uniquely African interpretations of studio portraiture.[40]

Malick Sidibé was born in Soloba, in southern Mali, and attended school in Bougouni, one hundred miles from Bamako. In 1952 he moved to Bamako to attend the École des Artisans Soudanais (School for Sudanese Craftsmen), now the Institut National des Arts (National Institute of Art), where he studied jewelry making. After graduating in 1955, he was hired by French photographer Gérard Guillat to decorate his shop, Photo Service. Guillat, known affectionately as *Gégé le pellicule*—literally, "Gégé the film"—later took him on as an apprentice. Sidibé started out doing basic studio jobs and gradually learned photography by watching the photographers at work.[41] He bought his first camera, a 6 x 9 Brownie Flash, in 1956, and began making portraits, mostly of Malian clients, for which Guillat gave him a share of the profits. In a recent interview Sidibé remarked that Guillat was there for the European trade whereas he was there for the African trade.[42]

In 1957 Sidibé began to do reportage—photographing events for private clients—in

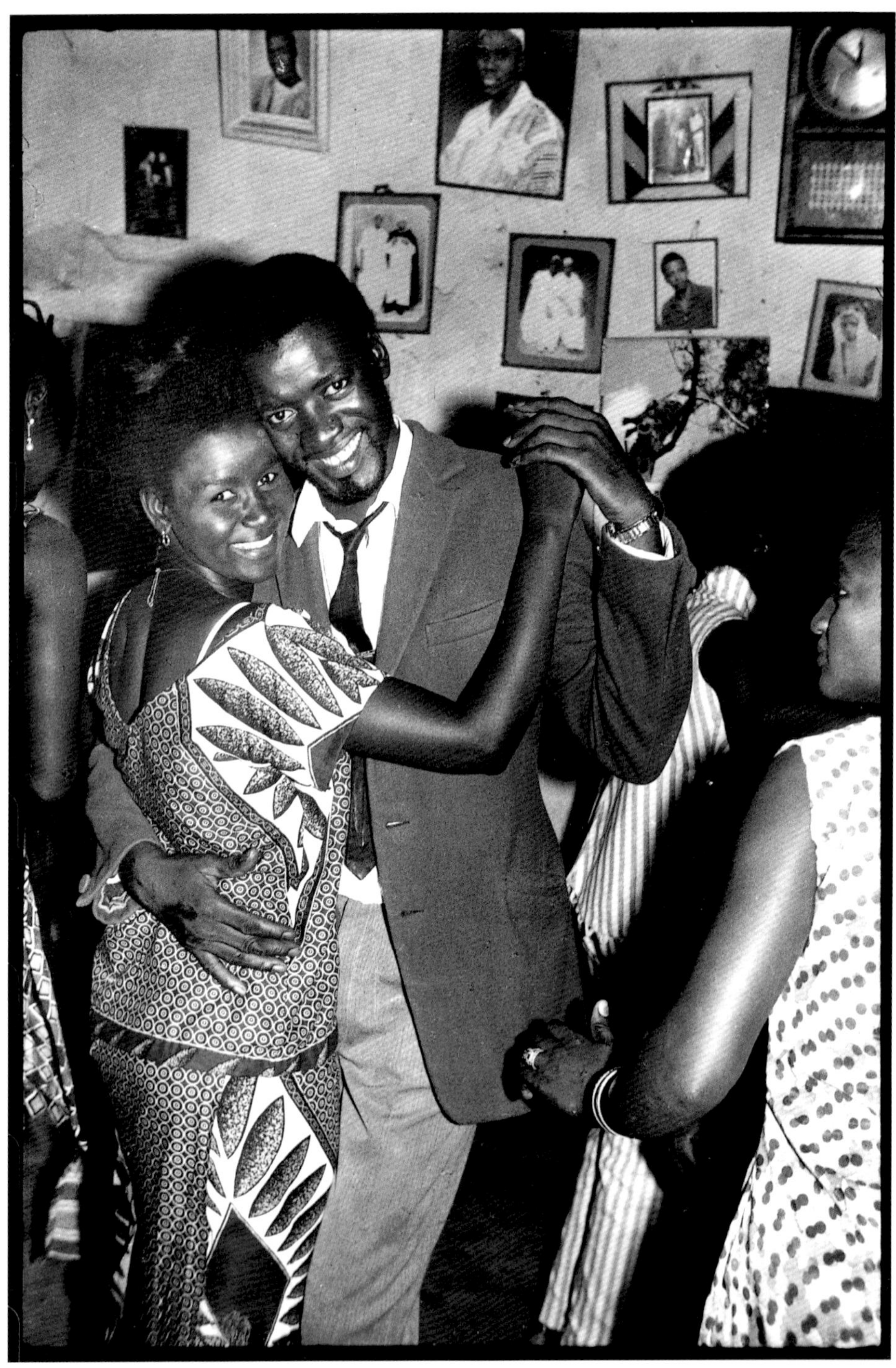

Fig. 12. Malick Sidibé, *A Couple of Dancers*, 1963. Gelatin silver print, 40 x 30 cm.

addition to portraits. Unlike his competitor Abderramane Sakaly, who specialized in photographing official events and activities of the upper class, Sidibé was hired by young people to photograph parties (fig. 12), club gatherings, and leisure activities, including Sunday outings by the Niger River. Sidibé has said that the young people of his time showed him that "when the moment is there you just have to live it ... you've got to live out those moments, especially when you're young and you haven't yet succumbed to the wisdom of adulthood, the sense of restraint that you develop, little by little, with age."[43] However, while he enjoyed the energetic atmosphere of the Bamako parties he was hired to photograph, Sidibé sees studio portraiture as a truer photographic art because he has more control over the resulting image. He likens the creation of a photographic portrait to working in other media: "For me, setting up a photo shoot isn't so different from drawing a scene: I decide what goes where, I decide how to pose the person in order to capture a certain physicality. That's what I do with cameras, with shadows and light. You know, I really think the art of photography is in the studio work."[44]

Guillat wanted Sidibé to take over Photo Service when he left Bamako in 1958, but the younger photographer did not feel experienced enough to do so. Two years later, however, he bought a full set of laboratory equipment from a man who was returning to France and opened Studio Malick at 30th Street, Corner 19, in Bagadadji, a neighborhood in the eastern part of Bamako.[45] Many of Guillat's clients stayed with him. Sidibé never advertised, preferring that his clients judge his talent by his work.[46] He notes that the stamp he used on the back of his photos served as publicity: "The kids who saw it were intrigued and came to Bagadadji. People said I was the best of the day!"[47] He also promoted his business with a 6 x 3-foot STUDIO MALICK sign in neon, which attracted many clients.[48]

Sidibé used an Agfa 6 x 6 camera with bellows and simple viewfinder, and a Foca Sport 35mm because it was less expensive. When photographing in the studio, he worked with slow speeds of 1/15 or 1/8 of a second to adjust for the dark skin of his clients. He had to be careful of any movement, which could ruin the shot or "make the person look tipsy."[49] As with Keïta's portraits, people preferred the smaller prints because they could put them in albums or mail them to friends. Prices had not changed dramatically from Keïta's day. A matte 9 x 13 print with serrated edges cost 100–150 CFAF and a glossy print 150–200—a significant expense given that the cost of a soft drink was only 15 CFAF.[50]

While portraits were his primary business, Sidibé continued to do reportage until the late 1970s. He has also been repairing cameras since 1957, and every inch of his studio continues to be taken up by cameras, camera parts, and other photographic equipment, as well as thousands of negatives stored in old Kodak paper boxes. Like other photographers of his generation, Sidibé found his practice undermined by the emergence of color photography in the 1980s. The excitement over colorful images and the availability of quick processing has lured most clients away from the tradition of black-and-white studio portraiture. Today there are businesses providing color processing on virtually every corner in Bamako. Sidibé's studio, however, continues to be an important neighborhood meeting place, a focal point of social life where information is exchanged. Although he takes few portraits today, the photographer is often found in front of his studio, with friends and visitors constantly shouting out greetings or dropping by to chat or sit quietly in the shade.

Sidibé opened his studio the same year that Keïta began working for the government. The two artists met for the first time on Keïta's wedding day in Bougouni, when Sidibé was still in school, but they did not develop a friendship until much later. Sidibé explains why:

> Here in Africa, there is a strong distrust of competition. Do you know what I mean? ... I am the younger photographer, and if I started showing up at his studio and then later on his business started to flounder, or the jobs stopped coming in, he might well think: "That young guy put a spell on me!" That's what always kept me from going over to his studio.[51]

Later, however, when Keïta needed his cameras repaired, he went to Sidibé, and a casual friendship began to develop. With the more recent exhibition of their work internationally, they have become better acquainted, and Sidibé often represents Keïta abroad, since the older photographer travels infrequently.

In the Studio

The portrait studio can be a place in which to create images that embody the accepted social ideal. But it can also allow sitters to break away from social norms and construct idealized individual identities, living out dreams and aspirations they cannot achieve in everyday life.[52] Photography thus offers sitters an opportunity to negotiate between how society defines them and how they wish to be defined.

The studio itself serves as a physical stage for the construction of a self-image. In Sidibé's studio, there is a narrow, raised platform on which his subjects often stand or sit. Powerful lamps emphasize a sense of theater, especially when they create strong shadows behind the subject. In many of Keïta's portraits, the backdrop that transformed the photographer's courtyard into a studio serves the function of a stage set.

In keeping with the theater analogy, the sitters become actors, performing for the camera.[53] As curator and critic Okwui Enwezor described it, "The sitters are the creators of their own personal image repertoire: who they are; who they want to become; what sort of mask to inhabit; and what prosthetic devices they need to achieve that look."[54] The photographer plays the role of director. He facilitates the creation of the desired image by providing clothing, accessories, and props; by creating an ambience through lighting and backdrop; and by arranging the sitter's pose and the composition of the photograph.

The standard portrait formats in Keïta's repertoire include close-up, bust, and full-length figures; seated, standing, and reclining figures; singles, couples, and groups. One of the more popular formats in his repertoire was the angled bust portrait, which the photographer says he invented.[55] In this pose, the sitter's face was captured in a three-quarter view, with the body appearing to lean toward the edge of the picture frame (cat. no. 29). In his full-length poses, female sitters lean against the back of a chair, resting their chin on their hand or looking back over their shoulder. In other cases, sitters cross their hands in their lap or hold them together at the side of their face in a prayerful pose. Subjects standing behind their companions often place hands awkwardly on the shoulders of the sitter (cat. no. 30). One pose in particular, in which the subject places one leg on a chair and rests an elbow on her knee, putting a hand or a finger to her face, appears to be an African innovation (cat. no. 31).

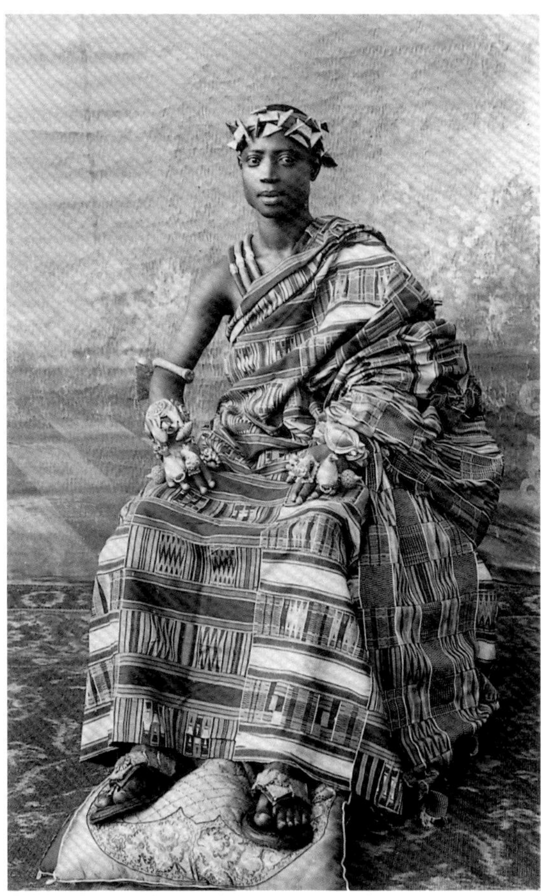

Fig. 13. Photographer unknown, *Nana Kwabene Wiafe II, Omanhene of Ofinsu, Ashanti, Gold Coast, BWA*, c. 1900–15. Postcard, gelatin silver print (cat. no. 9).

Another pose Keïta employed, also seen in several of the historical postcards mentioned above, has become the traditional means of presentation in formal portraits among the Yoruba of Nigeria, as photographer Steven Sprague notes in his 1975 study of photography in that culture.[56] The subject sits facing the camera or at a slight angle to it, with both feet on the ground, hands in his lap or on his knees, with legs apart, possibly to allow the proud display of clothing fabric. Frequently assumed at ceremonies and events, especially by older members of the community, the stance symbolizes prestige and social standing. Through his research, Sprague has determined that this pose does not appear in nineteenth- and twentieth-century British portrait photography. It seems to be rooted in depictions of African royalty, as evident in a postcard portrait of Nana Kwabene Wiafe II, Omanhene of Ofinsu, Ashanti, taken in the Gold Coast (now Ghana) in the early twentieth century (fig. 13). The omanhene, or leader, is seated with his feet on a pillow. The frontal position, resulting in the perfect symmetry of face and body, is

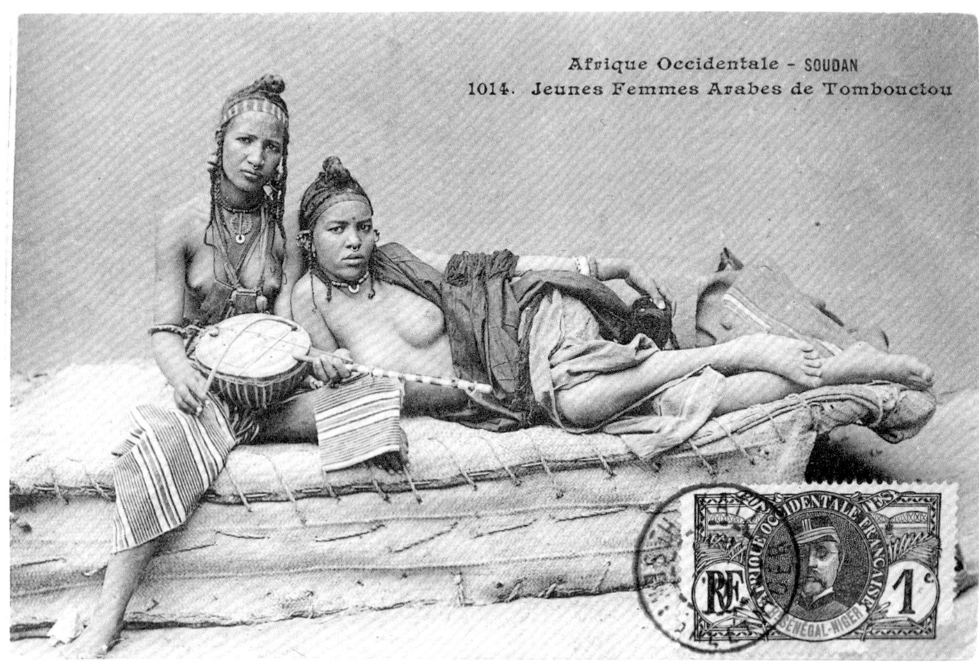

Fig. 14. François-Edmond Fortier, *Afrique Occidentale — Soudan, 1014. Jeunes Femmes Arabes de Tombouctou* [Young Arab women from Timbuktu, Mali], c. 1905. Postcard, collotype (cat. no. 10).

particularly important in court portraiture because, as anthropologist Michèle Couquet explains, it "imposes on the beholder of the king's effigy a privileged position of viewing, a single point of view, that of the face-to-face encounter."[57]

Keïta's photograph of two Haratine women from northern Mali portrays the subjects in this traditional pose (cat. no. 32). It is interesting to observe, however, that the somber dignity the pose connotes is offset by the smiling faces. Formally, the pose conveys both symmetry and balance. In another Keïta portrait, the symmetry of the pose is disrupted by the shifting of the subject's body off axis, and the placement of her elbow on the back of the chair (cat. no. 33). Still, the weight suggested by her clothing creates a solid three-dimensionality that balances the composition. This same pose surfaces in a 1975 Sidibé portrait of two friends (cat. no. 34). A young man in jeans sits stiffly, his hands resting on his knees. As in Keïta's portrait, the subject's head and body are angled toward the right, but in Sidibé's portrait, he sneaks a look at the photographer out of the corner of his eye.

Sidibé's portraits reflect a relaxation of photographic conventions that resulted from both the atmosphere surrounding independence and the youth movement of the 1960s. Conventional poses were largely discarded by both the photographer and the sitter, and more informal positions were adopted that reflected the modern world in which they lived.

As Sidibé said of his younger clientele, "With all their energy and frenzy, young people would strike any old funny or odd pose."[58]

For the most part Sidibé's photographs portray his sitters full-length, with heads facing forward. Groups of figures are symmetrically and centrally arranged, with some seated and others standing, or staggered to enhance effect. Sidibé also made bust-length portraits, particularly of young women wanting to show off their new hairstyles (cat. nos. 24 and 25). Although Sidibé's portraits are posed, it is clear that his sitters have actively participated in the choice of their stance, the placement of their arms, and the selection of props. Some figures stand with hands on hips, or slid jauntily into pockets (cat. no. 35). Others thrust their hips out and even appear to swagger (cat. no. 36). One man has himself photographed with his sheep and in another image, a little boy is flanked by paper flowers (cat. nos. 37 and 38). Cigarettes dangle from the mouths of musicians (cat. no. 39). Taking control over the act of being photographed, Sidibé's subjects seem to throw their personalities at the camera to announce their individuality.

Another pose that both Keïta and Sidibé may have adapted from postcard images is that of the reclining woman (cat. nos. 40 and 41). A recurring figure in postcards of Africa, the odalisque is represented in a Fortier postcard of two Arab women from Timbuktu, taken around 1905 (fig. 14). It is likely that themes such as this one were inspired by motifs first used in North Africa by visual artists and writers constructing images of the "Orient" for Western audiences.[59] The odalisque has a long history as a symbol of uncontrolled sexuality, serving in the Western imagination both to confirm the moral corruption of these "primitive" cultures and to nourish lustful longings.[60]

The portraits of Keïta and Sidibé, however, are a reinvention of that pose. The private commissioning and domestic nature of their photographs suggest that the odalisque is not there for the viewer, but for herself.[61] In Fortier's postcard, the women are depicted as objects; in the photographs of Keïta and Sidibé, the reclining woman is the subject, conveying her own self-image to the world. Manthia Diawara notes that the reclining pose indicates the subject's social status and is traditionally associated with an unmarried woman who invites a suitor to her home.[62] Yet in Keïta's image, the subject quietly enjoys tea for one. Sidibé suggests that this representation was chosen by the woman for her own personal reflection:

> [T]he subject ... can also create the image according to her own vision. Sometimes a woman comes to my studio and she wants her picture taken with a radio. Sometimes a woman comes looking for a more quiet, laid-back atmosphere, as if she were in her bedroom. If the photographer can sense what she wants, the end result can be very charming. There's a sort of serenity and ease, almost as if she were at home, not in a photography studio.[63]

The pose of the reclining woman exemplifies how a sitter transformed the studio into a theater where her own sense of self could be portrayed. At the same time it points to

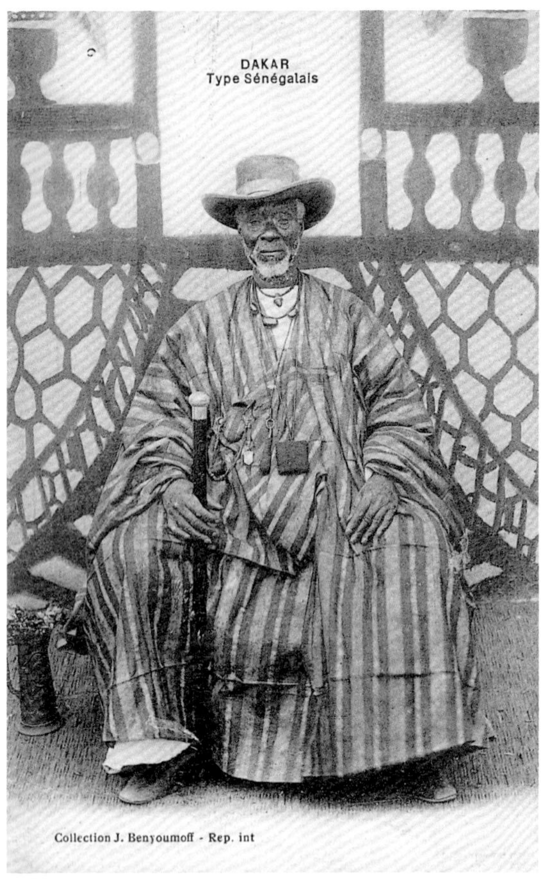

Fig. 15. J. Benyoumoff (distributor), *Dakar, Type Sénégalais* [Dakar, Senegalese Type], c. 1900–15. Postcard (cat. no. 11).

the conscious/subconscious application of earlier portrait motifs to African self-representation. The appropriation of these tropes by Africans on their own terms provides a powerful counter-narrative to colonialist history and to images of Africans made by Europeans and by Africans working under colonial influence.

While the photographers' role was to fulfill their sitters' wishes, they also asserted their artistic will. Keïta describes how his sitters selected the pose they wanted, but says he felt that he always knew which one was better. Ultimately he would convince the subject that a certain arrangement would result in the best image. Keïta said in an interview: "It's easy to take a photo, but what really made a difference was that I always knew how to find the right position, and I was never wrong. Their head slightly turned, a serious face, the position of the hands ... I was capable of making someone look really good."[64] Sidibé, like Keïta, said he knew what was necessary to produce a successful portrait:

> The photographer's relationship with his subject is established by touch. You had to arrange the person, find the right profile, light the face properly to catch the outlines and features, and find the right light to make the body look beautiful. I also used make-up. I used positions and attitudes that suited the person well. I had my own tactics.[65]

Backdrops also play a pivotal role in the appearance of the portrait, by isolating the subject from distracting environmental details, reducing the depth of field, and allowing the photographer to control the mise-en-scène and frame the composition. In European studio portraiture, painted backdrops created fictional settings, such as interiors and street scenes, that suggested a location and narrative, as well as adding a decorative element to the portrait.[66] Early studios run by African photographers catering to the urban elite continued the convention of painted backdrops of pastoral gardens and interior settings with Western-style architectural details such as columns and arches. Local artists also reinterpreted European subjects in their own painting style, as in a Senegalese postcard (fig. 15) in which the backdrop, depicting a staircase with balustrade and urns, is painted in a rough, spontaneous style. This is an example of European conventions becoming part of the vernacular. Eventually African artists eliminated European subjects altogether and painted scenes of African towns or architecture, such as mosques.[67] Both European and African photographers also used makeshift backdrops of plain or patterned cloth.

Keïta mounted backdrops of decorative textiles against the wall of his courtyard to take his outdoor portraits. He used backdrops because, he has been quoted as saying, "you couldn't put the clients in front of a white wall: it's not respectful."[68] Keïta's backdrops of patterned textiles are an important element of his aesthetic. The first was his own bedspread (cat. no. 42), made of a lacy material, which he used from 1948 to 1951. After 1952 Keïta changed his backdrop every two or three years, employing a series of textiles—one with small flowers, another with a leaf motif, a third with an arabesque pattern, and the last a solid dark cloth curtain. When patterned textiles are used, the figures tend to merge with the decorative setting. In Keïta's portraits the print of the sitter's clothing occasionally clashes with the backdrop to create a graphic explosion of pattern and design (cat. no. 33).

Sidibé employed a striped backdrop to achieve a similar effect. One visual extravaganza is a combination of stripes, plaid, flowers, and diamonds (cat. no. 15). Sidibé sometimes used a plain curtain or blank wall that would not divert attention from his subjects' clothing and skin tone. However, in his portraits there is almost always a pattern of some kind on the floor of the studio, which adds a decorative effect to the image without distracting the viewer from the sitter's face (cat. no. 43).[69]

Because Keïta took most of his photographs in the courtyard of his home, the bare ground is usually visible. While the backdrop creates the illusion of a studio, this foreground points out the artificiality of the constructed environment (cat. no. 44). A similar effect occurs in several of Sidibé's portraits when the camera is pulled back far enough to reveal objects of everyday life outside the constructed space of the studio set (cat. no. 45). Still, this effect does not distract the sitters and photographer from the formality of the portrait session or the care taken with the sitters' appearance and the posing of the picture.

The range of props and accessories that assist with the staging of the portrait is similar in studios across West Africa. Among the objects in Keïta's studio were several types of chairs, handbags, radios, a telephone, an alarm clock, a scooter, a bicycle, a pedestal with tablecloth, plastic flowers, European suits, pocket handkerchiefs, jewelry, watches, and fountain pens. The same props were used over and over again: for example, in several bust-length portraits of young men, the sitters wear the same tie, glasses, and watch and are equipped with the same pocket handkerchief and pen. However, it is not always clear which accessories belonged to the sitter and which belonged to the studio. Clients often brought their own possessions, such as bicycles, for inclusion in their portraits (cat. no. 46). Women sometimes came to Keïta's studio with several changes of clothing. Certainly the sheep in Sidibé's portrait of a man named Tauré was not one of the photographer's studio props! In the 1960s and 1970s Sidibé's clientele used accessories and embellishments less frequently. Both photographer and sitters preferred a starker studio space, but he still offered props such as radios, flowers, jewelry, shoulder bags, and handbags.

Photographers are experienced in the creation of appearance. In Mali, sitters choose a photographer not just for his technical skills, but for his knowledge of fashion and style, his ability to interpret social values, and his inventiveness in helping the sitter create a particular identity.[70] Sidibé uses humor to relax people and put them in a good mood. He believes that "a good photographer is also a social animal. Do good work, and people love you.... Because the customers don't really see the camera, they see you, the artist—you become the product they're buying. For them, the photographer has the power to make them more beautiful—that's your role."[71]

Costume and accessories provide extrinsic details that assist in the construction of images reflecting the social roles of sitters and emphasizing the subjects' beauty, wealth, cosmopolitanism, and modernity. The visual codes identifying Keïta's and Sidibé's subjects were embedded in hairstyle, clothing style, textile patterns, scarification, jewelry, and props. While the meaning of these codes may not be immediately apparent to the outside viewer, they are used in everyday communication to signal social standing or affiliation with a group, as well as an individual identity.

Sometimes the group itself, such as a family unit, was portrayed in the photograph. A portrait might emphasize the importance of a subject's position as the head of the household, as in Keïta's photograph of a civil servant with his wife and children (cat. no. 47). Another Keïta image expresses the power of the maternal role (cat. no. 48). Although the role of family is less pronounced in Sidibé's portraits, his image of a couple and their child posing on a motorbike expresses familial love and support (cat. no. 49). The wife rests her hand affectionately on her husband's shoulder while their baby grasps the handlebars in imitation of his father.

In individual portraits, some sitters indicated their role in the community by incorporating accessories, such as a sewing machine, camera, gun, boxing gloves, or a musical instrument, to reflect their profession. Tailors, photographers, hunters, military men, teachers, boxers, and musicians abound in both artists' work (cat. nos. 39 and 50–55). In one particularly striking example by Sidibé, a tailor suggests his level of skill and creativity by having himself photographed with a headless mannequin wearing a white wedding gown (cat. no. 56).

Women in Keïta's and Sidibé's portraits were particularly interested in identifying themselves with beauty and wealth through the display of clothing, jewelry, and hairstyles. Aminata Dramane Traoré, Mali's minister of

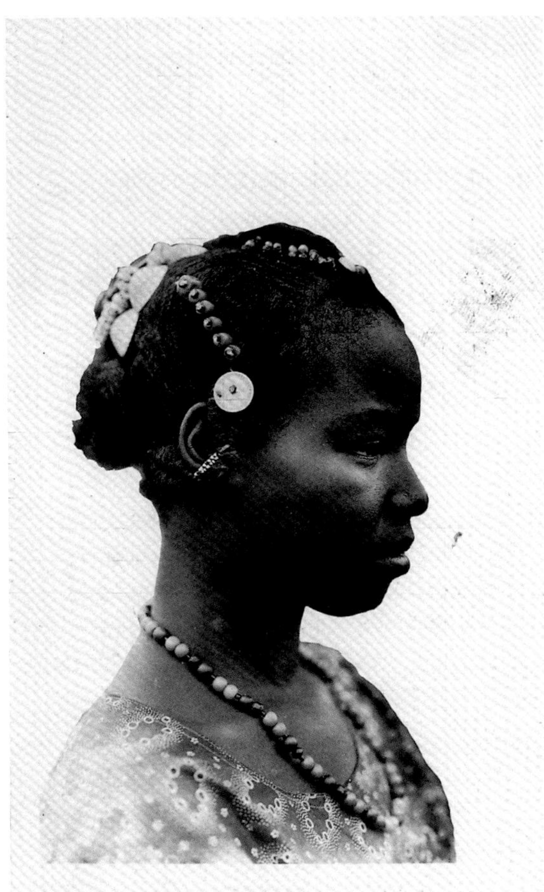

Fig. 16. G. Lerat, *35. A.O.F. — Hte. Volta, Jeunes Toucouleurs* [Upper Volta, Young Toucouleurs], c. 1900–15. Postcard (cat. no. 12).

culture and tourism, has written that "clothing is the bearer of our, and society's, images of ourselves, of our desires and impulses."[72] Keïta recalls:

> What was important was that their jewels appeared in the photos. They wore elaborate jewelry: earrings sometimes big enough to decorate the whole studio, rings, hairpieces, and bracelets in gold, coral, or amber ... all these details, external signs of wealth, beauty and elegance, were of great importance.[73]

Long, slender fingers on women were also seen as signs of beauty, elegance, and high social standing. A young woman portrayed by Keïta wears a ring, a gold choker with a flower design, a carnelian necklace, and a series of gold earrings along the edge of her ear, as well as gold buttons and other decorations in her hair (cat. no. 57). Not only do these adornments accentuate her beauty, but they also indicate that she comes from a family of some affluence. For Sidibé's subjects traditional adornments were less important than being photographed with objects of consumer culture and contemporary fashion, such as shoes, watches, and shoulder bags.

Across Africa the decoration and manipulation of hair has for centuries been an important means of communicating culture, social status, religious function, ethnic origin, phase of life cycle, and personal taste (see fig. 16 and cat. no. 58). In some of Keïta's photographs of children, heads are shaved in various patterns to indicate family or tribe, and small patches of hair are left at the fontanel, the soft area of unfused bones in the skull, to prevent dangerous spirits from entering. Headscarves, obligatory for all married women, were signs of glamour and prestige and communicated information in the way they were worn. One style, "à la Versailles," was named after the car that has been used as a taxi in Bamako since the 1950s (cat. no. 31).[74]

In the 1960s and 1970s, hairstyles for women, such as braids, replaced headscarves. Often named after people, influential objects, or special events, they were linked more to fashion than to the traditional meanings they originally held, which varied from culture to culture. Still, stylists were able to perpetuate earlier traditions by reproducing and updating ancient hairstyles. Complex coiffures reflected a sitter's high social status and evoked admiration. Sidibé indicates that some clients came to his studio to be photographed every time they changed their hairstyle, which was an expensive and lengthy process. Several of his portraits capture the elaborate nature of these coiffures and the pride and excitement with which women wore them (cat. nos. 24, 25, and 59).[75]

Textiles are also a very important means of expression, although meanings vary from place to place. Patterns are related to words or phrases and therefore communicate specific messages aside from their visual impact. Often tailors and photographers had their shops side-by-side because both played the role of image-maker. Textile patterns, usually designed by women, offer critical, ironic, or humorous commentary dealing with men and women or political events.[76] For example, in a Keïta portrait of two women with their children, both women wear a fabric with a print called "the jealous dark eyes of my co-wife" (cat. no. 60), suggesting that even though the sharing of husbands is culturally and socially condoned, feelings of jealousy and rivalry are common among wives. A white-spotted print called "I'm not afraid of my co-wife's goggling eyes" reflects the same theme.[77] The number of pieces of fabric used or worn was also an indicator of wealth. The photographer "has to work with clothing," Sidibé remarked, "even down to the type of fabrics people wear. Certain fabrics look classy and can make the lady look very fancy."[78]

Both clothing and props in the portraits demonstrate the mixing of cultures that was Bamako's self-conscious embrace of modernity. The tastes and aspirations of consumers in urban areas were frequently shaped by Western ideas and goods introduced into Africa during and after the colonial era. Extensive cultural borrowing and reinterpretation resulted in the creation of local, African styles. In reference to Sidibé's work, Diawara has aptly described this as a diaspora aesthetic resulting from "an encounter between pre-Atlantic-slavery Africa, the post-civil rights American culture, and the post independence youth in Bamako."[79]

This mixing of cultures is evident in a Keïta portrait of a man dressed in a European suit complete with white shirt, bow tie, and pocket handkerchief, whose distinguishing facial scars provide a striking contrast to the large black-framed glasses he wears (cat. no. 29). This attraction to Western fashion does not reflect a longing to be Western, however, but rather a wish to be associated with contemporary trends and fashions (cat. no. 61). As one scholar has pointed out in regard to Keïta's subjects, "A spirited desire to shape one's image after those we deem more glamorous and celebrated than ourselves pays little attention to the distinction between colonizer and colonized, and is as much a part of Parisian life as Bamakois life."[80]

Still, according to Sidibé, the West had greater prestige:

> A simple watch or a tie around a man's neck, these things say that he's someone with

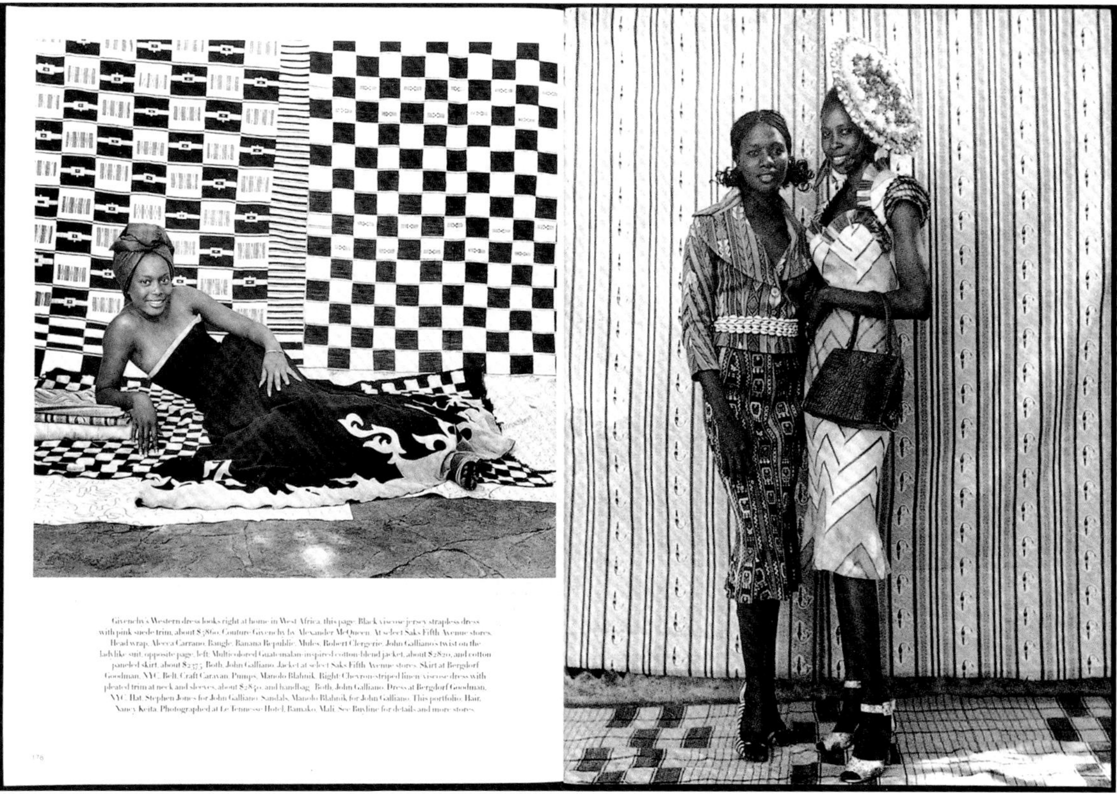

Fig. 17. Seydou Keïta, magazine spread from "Sunday Best," *Harper's Bazaar* (May 1998) (cat no. 73).

financial means, someone important. It's like when I was young, and there were kids who could afford to go to Paris—to Saint-Germain-des-Prés even! Sometimes, you could find the same clothes ... at one of the boutiques here in Bamako, but it's always far more impressive if it comes from Paris. Kids are like that.... Especially in those days, the mere fact that it came from the West gave the wearer a certain kind of power, a kind of power that kids are looking for. Grown men, too, I suppose.[81]

Keita expressed mixed feelings about the use of Western apparel and appurtenances: "We began to lose our ancestors' culture."[82] Despite his dismay at the loss of tradition, he provided European-style suits to clients who desired them for portrait sessions.

Although it was acceptable for men to wear Western suits and ties, during Keïta's time women bore the responsibility for preserving traditional dress. Very few of his female subjects are portrayed in contemporary Western clothing (cat. no. 62). However, with national independence and the liberation of the young in the 1960s and 1970s, more women chose Western clothing, including miniskirts and bell-bottoms, even though they risked punishment from their more traditional parents (cat. nos. 16, 22, and 63). Sidibé observed that "Every time there is a new fashion in dresses, [women] come to get their picture taken. Every time they get new shoes—everything! For women, particularly in an era when the media are everywhere, fashion is a very strong force."[83] Sidibé's portraits make it clear that young men also evinced a love of fashion and an excitement at demonstrating their urban chic (cat. nos. 15, 64, and 65). Sidibé sees fashionable clothes as evidence of buying power, for those who could afford them, and observed that no matter what country something came from, people wore it.[84]

The bicycles, motorcycles, radios, and telephones used as props were another expression of modernity. In Keïta's day, signifiers of wealth began to shift from traditional adornment to Western accoutrements. In one portrait a young man displays his wristwatch while leaning casually on a radio, which he pretends to adjust (cat. no. 66). For added effect, an alarm clock is perched on top of the radio. A Sidibé portrait depicts a group of Peul shepherds posing awkwardly with a radio (cat. no. 67). Other portraits show subjects posing with motor scooters and motorbikes (cat. nos. 68 and 69). Even if objects such as these were merely studio props, the sitters expected to be identified with what they signified—visible proof of social success and urbanity. Photography allowed those who were not well placed socially or financially the means to experiment with these expressions of modernity.

Sometimes sitters openly emulated characters from Western culture. For example, male subjects presented themselves as dandies in the style of French symbolist poets such as Mallarmé, whose work was read by schoolteachers and students in the 1950s (cat. no.

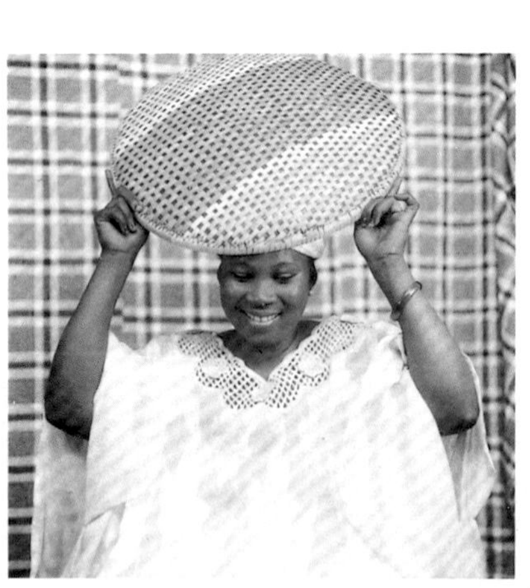

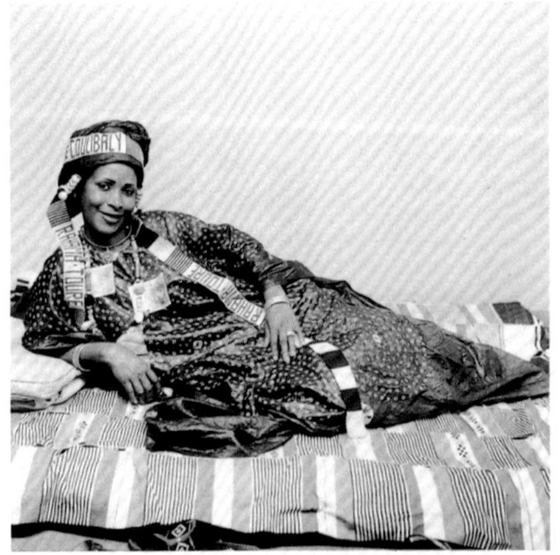

Fig. 18. Malick Sidibé, photo spread published as "Avoir 33 ans à Bamako," *Double, nouveau féminin* 004 (February/March 2000) (cat. no. 74).

70).[85] Others took on established characters they identified with from films that came to Bamako, which had its first movie theater in 1910, soon after electricity became available.[86] Sidibé and others have observed that young people imitated the style and attitudes of actors such as Eddie Constantine, an American who played tough-guy Lemmy Caution, Federal Agent Number One, in French films in the 1950s. The central figure in a Keïta portrait of three young men wears a half-open shirt and a hat pushed high on his head in the style of Lemmy Caution (cat. no. 71). In Sidibé's portraits, sitters present themselves as hipsters sporting wide-brim hats and Mexican sombreros, cigarettes and sunglasses, aspiring to be rock stars like their idols, James Brown and the Beatles (cat. no. 36). These were personas, acted out by the subjects and understood by the viewer to be part of a performance.[87] As Malian sociologist Youssouf Tata Cissé has confirmed, to be photographed was a way not only of affirming your own identity, but also of playing the star with whom you identified; aside from Lemmy Caution, there was Kassidy, "the king of the most terrible Texan cowboys."[88]

In the 1960s, as the conventions of photographic portraiture became more flexible, clients took a more active role in deciding how they wanted to be represented. This relaxing of portrait conventions in terms of both formal elements and the traditional roles of photographer and sitter is connected in part to a stronger focus on individuality as a result of modernization and migration from rural to urban areas. Young people who moved to the city escaped the constraints of social and familial obligations. They had the freedom to smoke, go to movies, wear what they wanted, save their earnings, and choose their own spouse. Sidibé has noted that music as well as fashion enabled young people "to experience a different kind of freedom."[89] Initially Keïta's subjects constructed a role for themselves that conformed to societal norms. A portrait offered proof that one was fulfilling one's role in society. Later, as reflected in the work of Sidibé, subjects refused to define themselves through their social role in the community. Women in their bathing suits and young men in jeans and sunglasses convey this rebellion (cat. no. 72).

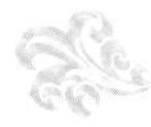

Keïta's and Sidibe's most recent work, produced for internationally distributed fashion magazines, includes images made in the style of their earlier studio portraits. Keïta has photographed for *Harper's Bazaar* young Bamakois women in textiles and styles based in part on African dress (fig. 17). Sidibé meanwhile has completed a portrait series that was published in *Double, nouveau féminin* (fig. 18).[90] In the case of Keïta's photographs, the emphasis is on fashion—the models are there to support the real subject, which is the clothing. Although Keïta continues to employ the tools of backdrop and pose, such as that of the reclining woman, these works are not portraits.

Sidibé's photographs for *Double*, a French fashion magazine, are more ambiguous. The photographer builds on the formulas of his earlier work to create images in which fashion and individual portrait use are merged. While his subjects are likely aware of the ultimate purpose of the photographs, their warm smiles reflect a continuing interaction with the photographer that is not evident in Keïta's photographs in *Harper's*. As with the large-scale exhibition prints, the subjects of these recent works remain anonymous as the intention and mode of presentation shifts to meet the needs of a completely different audience.

Keïta's and Sidibé's portrait photographs, originally printed in a small, postcard-size format for private use and now exhibited and sold as large-scale prints, have become part of a larger critical discourse surrounding contemporary photography. For example, in "Home from Home: Portraits from Places in Between," Kobena Mercer analyzes the work of Keïta in relation to that of his contemporary Mama Casset of Senegal and several artists active today to explore how photography has enabled African and black artists to take control of their own representation.[91] With the different modes of presentation in which their work is now viewed and the resulting interpretations by a variety of audiences, the photographs have taken on a life of their own. Still, although both photographers are creating new work specifically for audiences and markets outside Africa, it is important to remember that they began as commercial photographers and that their photographs are based on a tradition of portrait photography with deep roots in West African history and culture. It is from those roots that they draw their power.

Notes

1. Keïta remarked that the first time he saw his photographs at exhibition size, it was almost as if the subjects were standing right in front of him, "in the flesh." It was then that he knew he had done good work (Seydou Keïta, interview by the author, Bamako, 15 November 2000).

2. Philippe Salaün, a French photographer, related a story about being invited to have a meal with a Malian family in Bamako. He noticed that a portrait on the living-room wall had the same backdrop and accessories as the prints he had recently been making from negatives by an African photographer. The image turned out to be a photograph by Keïta. The family was unaware of Keïta's international renown. To them, the photograph was simply a portrait of their mother—a souvenir of her. (Philippe Salaün, conversation with the author, Paris, 17 November 2000.)

3. Martha Rosler, "Lookers, Buyers, Dealers, and Makers: Thoughts on Audience," in *Art After Modernism: Rethinking Representation,* ed. Brian Wallis (New York, 1984), 333.

4. See André Magnin, ed., *Seydou Keïta* (Zurich/Berlin/New York, 1997) and *Malick Sidibé* (Zurich/Berlin/New York, 1998); Elizabeth Bigham, "Issues of Authorship in the Portrait Photographs of Seydou Keïta," *African Arts* 32 (Spring 1999): 56–67, 94–96; Robert Storr, "Bamako: Full Dress Parade," *Parkett* 49 (1997): 24–34; Manthia Diawara, "Talk of the Town," *Artforum* 36 (1998): 64–71 and "The 1960s in Bamako: Malick Sidibé and James Brown," The Andy Warhol Foundation for the Visual Arts, Paper Series on the Arts, Culture and Society, no. 11 (2001).

5. For more on this topic, see Elizabeth Edwards, ed., *Anthropology and Photography, 1860–1920* (New Haven and London, 1992) and Okwui Enwezor and Octavio Zaya, "Colonial Imaginary, Tropes of Disruption: History, Culture, and Representation in the Works of African Photographers," in Okwui Enwezor, Olu Oguibe, and Octavio Zaya, *In/sight: African Photographers, 1940 to the Present,* exh. cat., Solomon R. Guggenheim Museum (New York, 1996).

6. Keïta, interview by André Magnin, in *Seydou Keïta*, 12.

7. Keïta, interview by the author.

8. Sidibé, interview by André Magnin, in *Malick Sidibé*, 38.

9. Malick Sidibé, interview by the author, Bamako, 13 November 2000.

10. Keïta, interview by Magnin, 11.

11. One such photographer was Augustus Washington, an African American who emigrated to Liberia, where he established a portrait studio. He also traveled to other

coastal countries to take portrait photographs. Ann M. Shumard, *A Durable Memento: Portraits by Augustus Washington, African American Daguerreotypist,* exh. cat., National Portrait Gallery, Smithsonian Institution (Washington, D.C., 1999).

12. For overviews and approaches to the study of the history of photography in Africa, see Pascal Martin Saint-Léon, N'Goné Fall, and Frédérique Chapuis, eds., *Anthology of African and Indian Ocean Photography* (Paris, 1999); Enwezor, Oguibe, and Zaya, *In/sight*; Tobias Wendl and Heike Behrend, eds., *Snap Me One!: Studiofotografen in Afrika* (Munich, 1998); and *Porträt Afrika: Fotografische Positionen eines Jahrhundert* (Berlin, 2000).

13. David Prochaska, "Fantasia of the Photothèque: French Postcard Views of Colonial Senegal," *African Arts* 24 (October 1991): 40.

14. Vera Viditz-Ward, "Studio Photography in Freetown," in *Anthology,* 36.

15. Christraud M. Geary, "Different Visions?: Postcards from Africa by European and African Photographers and Sponsors," in *Delivering Views: Distant Cultures in Early Postcards,* ed. Christraud M. Geary and Virginia-Lee Webb (Washington, D.C., 1998), 147–77.

16. Geary, "Different Visions?,"154.

17. Like the commercial postcards, however, the contemporary exhibition prints created from Keïta's and Sidibé's negatives move the images from their original, intimate contexts into the public realm, where anonymous sitters are viewed by equally anonymous audiences. But whereas the commercially distributed postcards treated the sitters as "types," the contemporary prints treat the images as "art," subject to the formal expectations Westerners bring to museums.

18. Agnès de Gouvion Saint-Cyr, "Africa of Gods, Africa of People," in *Anthology,* 19.

19. Erika Nimis, "The Golden Age of Black-and-White in Mali," in *Anthology,* 105.

20. Heike Behrend and Tobias Wendl, "Afrika in den Bildern seiner Studiofotografen," in *Snap Me One!,* 15.

21. Tobias Wendl, "Portraits and Scenery," in *Anthology,* 143.

22. M.-L. Villien-Rossi, "Bamako, capitale du Mali," *Bulletin de l'Institut Fondamental d'Afrique Noire* 28, série B (1966): 249–96; Claude Meillassoux, *Urbanization of an African Community: Voluntary Associations in Bamako* (Seattle, 1968), 3–40.

23. *Monographie du District de Bamako* (Bamako, 1994), 22.

24. Garnier has indicated that the first photographer in Bamako was a Monsieur Merle, who had a studio near the European cemetery. Erika Nimis, *Photographes de Bamako de 1935 à nos jours* (Paris, 1998), 14.

25. Sidibé, interview by the author.

26. Dimensions are in centimeters unless otherwise noted.

27. Keïta, interview by the author.

28. Tièmòkò Keïta, interview by André Magnin, in *Seydou Keïta,* 17.

29. Youssouf Tata Cissé, *Seydou Keïta* (Paris, 1995), n.p.

30. Keïta, interview by the author.

31. Because there was no electricity in more rural areas, when Keïta traveled to take photographs for identification cards, he converted a petrol barrel into a darkroom and used a kerosene lamp to develop his prints (Keïta, interview by Magnin, 11).

32. Keïta, interview by the author.

33. None of Keïta's work from 1935 to around 1947 appears to have survived, although the artist suggests that he may one day find the photographs in his studio (Keïta, interview by Magnin, 13).

34. Ibid., 10.

35. Ibid.

36. Martine Ravache, "Un photographe et son appareil, Seydou Keïta," *Photographies Magazine* 78 (July–August 1996): 66.

37. Keïta, interview by the author.

38. Keïta, interview by Magnin, 11.

39. Most of the photographers of the time made contact prints with a 13 x 18 negative, which was the standard, since it was expensive to buy an enlarger and impossible to use it when traveling.

40. Jean-François Werner and Erika Nimis have pointed out similarities among African studio photographers of the 1950s and 1960s in learning experience, professional status, aesthetic rules, technique, and studio design and setup. In addition to backdrops and props, most photographers used similar equipment and the same aperture and exposure time. Jean-François Werner and Erika Nimis,

"Zur Geschichte der Fotografie im frankophonen Westafrika," in *Snap Me One!*, 20.

41. Sidibé, interview by Magnin, 35.

42. Sidibé, interview by Hubert Filser and Peter Stepan, "La grande fête du photographe: Entretien avec Malick Sidibé," in *Porträt Afrika*, 34.

43. Sidibé, interview by the author.

44. Ibid.

45. Sidibé, interview by Magnin, 36. Sidibé also did portrait work outside of the studio and was occasionally invited to clients' homes to take pictures of the family, or traveled to rural areas to take identification photos.

46. Sidibé, interview by the author.

47. Sidibé, interview by Magnin, 39.

48. Ibid., 38.

49. Ibid., 39.

50. Sidibé, interview by Filser and Stepan, 34.

51. Sidibé, interview by the author.

52. Behrend and Wendl, "Afrika in den Bildern seiner Studiofotografen," 13.

53. See Bigham, "Issues of Authorship," for a discussion of the subjects' role in the creation of their portraits.

54. Okwui Enwezor, interview by Michael Thoss, "Spotted Vision: An Interview with Okwui Enwezor," *Porträt Afrika*, 19.

55. Keïta, interview by Magnin, 11. Mama Casset, a contemporary of Keïta's in Senegal, was known for a similar format.

56. Steven F. Sprague, "Yoruba Photography: How the Yoruba See Themselves," *African Arts* 12 (November 1978): 52–59, 107.

57. Michèle Couquet, *African Royal Court Art* (Chicago and London, 1998), 57.

58. Sidibé, interview by Magnin, 39.

59. Literary historian Edward Said coined the term "Orientalism" to describe the cultural phenomenon of representations of Middle Eastern subjects produced for Western audiences. See Edward Said, *Orientalism* (New York, 1978).

60. See Malek Alloula, *The Colonial Harem* (Minneapolis, 1986), for a provocative discussion of postcards of women in Algeria taken by European photographers.

61. Robert Storr makes a similar observation regarding one of Keïta's photographs. Storr, "Bamako," 26.

62. Diawara, "Talk of the Town," 68.

63. Sidibé, interview by the author.

64. Keïta, interview by Magnin, 11.

65. Sidibé, interview by Magnin, 39.

66. See Lucy Lippard, "Frames of Mind," *Afterimage* 24 (March/April 1997): 8–12. This issue of *Afterimage*, "From the Background to the Foreground: The Photo Backdrop and Cultural Expression," is devoted to the use of painted backdrops, props, and accessories in portrait photography.

67. For about a year, Sidibé used a backdrop of a mosque painted by a Senegalese artist, but he was unhappy with the results (Sidibé, interview by the author). Recently backdrops have evolved even further. Some depict living rooms full of electronic equipment, to suggest wealth and luxury, or modern means of transportation, such as cars and planes, to convey the idea that the subject is traveling to a different place and time. This is especially popular in Ghana, as is apparent in the work of Philip Kwame Apagya. See *Anthology* for examples.

68. Margaret Loke, "Inside Photography," *The New York Times*, 11 July 1997, C23.

69. Occasionally Keïta also placed a patterned textile or rug on the ground in addition to the backdrop.

70. Jean-Loup Pivin, "The Icon and the Totem," in *Anthology*, 26.

71. Sidibé, interview by the author.

72. Aminata Dramane Traoré, "African Fashion: A Message," in *The Art of African Fashion*, ed. Els van der Plas and Marlous Willensen (The Hague/Trenton, N. J./Asmara, Eritrea, 1998), 8.

73. Keïta, interview by Magnin, 13.

74. Magnin, *Seydou Keïta*, 280.

75. Since the late 1960s Nigerian photographer J. D. 'Okhai Ojeikere has focused on the diversity and beauty of hairstyles in Nigeria. See André Magnin, *J. D. 'Okhai Ojeikere: Photographies* (Paris, 2000).

76. This knowledge is complicated by the fact that many textiles are designed and manufactured outside of Africa.

For a discussion of the relationship between photography and textiles, see Kerstin Pinther, "'Wenn die Ehe eine Erdnuß wäre ...' Uber Textilien und Fotografie in Afrika," in *Snap Me One!*, 36–41.

77. Magnin, *Seydou Keïta*, 273, 275.

78. Sidibé, interview by the author.

79. Diawara, "The 1960s in Bamako," 21. Diawara asserts that the young people captured in Sidibé's images of parties and other social events saw studio photography as old-fashioned, reserved for people pretending to be Bamakois, but his portraits of sitters in bell-bottoms and miniskirts discussed here suggest otherwise.

80. Ruth Kerkham, "Double Stitched: Colonial Pattern Making in the Works of Seydou Keïta and Yinka Shonibare," paper presented at College Art Association annual meeting, Chicago, March 2001.

81. Sidibé, interview by the author.

82. Keïta, interview by Magnin, 12.

83. Sidibé, interview by the author.

84. Ibid.

85. Diawara, "Talk of the Town," 70.

86. Meillassoux, *Urbanization*, 8.

87. Enwezor, interview by Thoss, 19.

88. Cissé, *Seydou Keïta*, n.p.

89. Sidibé, interview by the author.

90. Eve MacSweeney, "Sunday Best," *Harper's Bazaar* (May 1998): 172–79; "Avoir 33 ans à Bamako," *Double, nouveau féminin* 004 (February/March 2000): n.p.

91. Kobena Mercer, "Home from Home: Portraits from Places in Between," in *Self Evident*, exh. cat., Ikon Gallery (Birmingham, England, 1995), n. p.

"Whenever I look at my negatives I feel proud of the work I've done.... Frankly, we work in order to earn our daily bread here. When you're the head of the household it's your job to make sure you can feed your family! Photography started out as a means to an end for me ... [but] I fell head over heels in love with photography, and it's been a lasting affair."

Seydou Keïta, Bamako, Mali, 15 November 2000

Interview by Michelle Lamunière, with the assistance of Baba Maiga
Translated from the French by Lia Brozgal

ML: *How did you come to learn photography?*

SK: My first job was actually in carpentry, making furniture out of wood. Starting at a very early age, I spent many hours with my father building furniture. So I came by the craft quite naturally; we built all kinds of furniture together—armoires, side-tables, chairs. Instead of going to school, I stayed home with my father and made little drums out of wood. When I was about twelve years old one of my uncles went to see his uncle in Dakar, Senegal. His father—my grandfather—lived there, too, and every year my uncle would go and stay for two months or so. On this one particular occasion, he came back from his trip with a tiny, boxlike contraption that he'd gotten as a gift from his uncle. On top there was a lever; inside, a place to put a roll of film. As soon as I saw it, I begged my uncle to tell me who it was for—hoping that it was for me. At first he said that his uncle had given it to him as a gift, but when he saw my enthusiasm he gave me the little box, along with a roll of film, and for the first time ever I tried my hand at photography.

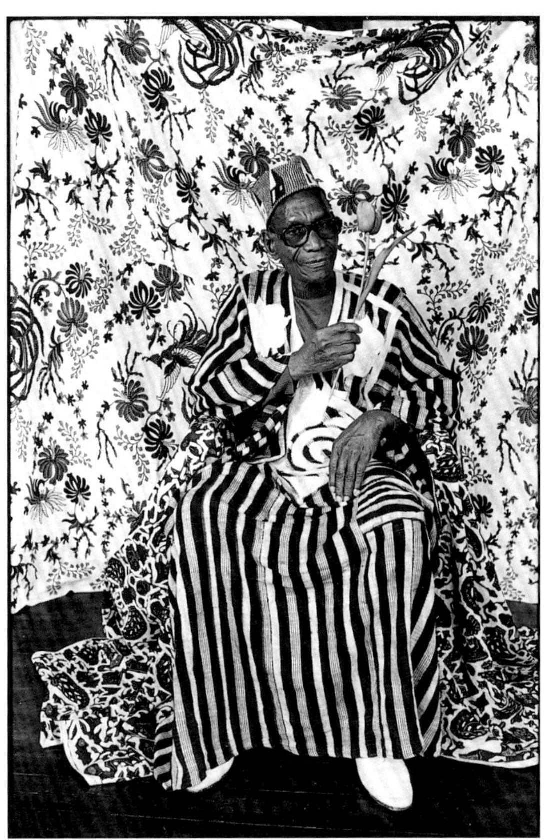

Françoise Huguier, *Seydou Keïta*, 1990s.

For my first roll of film I had no idea what I was doing! There was a European man here named Pierre Garnier who developed all of my pictures. When he saw the negatives from the first roll, all he could say was: "Oh boy, these exposures aren't too good." But I asked him to go ahead and print the photos anyway, so that I could see my own work. When I saw the printed frames, though, they were really bad. Garnier told me that with the camera that I was using I'd wear myself out by the time I figured out how to take proper photos. That camera had three speeds, and once I figured it out, then I was really able to start work. At the time, Pierre, who had all the necessary chemicals at his studio, sold me the developer liter by liter, and I began learning how to develop my own film. He also gave me some good advice as to how to take better pictures, simple things such as just keeping my hands still while shooting the photos. Everything fell into place with his suggestions, and I started to do nice work. I fell head over heels in love with photography, and it's been a lasting affair.

That was how it began, even though I continued to do carpentry. Actually, I combined the two activities; my first pictures were of the many apprentices who worked in the atelier with us. One day when I stopped in to see Pierre, he proposed that I try a different camera, a better one than that one I'd been using. He seemed to think that I was making more work for myself by using such a low-quality piece of equipment. According to him, if I was going to make any progress, I had to get a new camera. I also bought a converter that holds the film in a certain place. I started with 9 x 12 film and a converter with a frame, and that's how I shot all of the portraits. When you go to take the picture, you close the converter and then remove it, putting back the matte glass. Without knowing much to begin with, I can honestly say that I figured it all out on my own, and I continued to work with that camera until 1949. Of course, I took a lot of bad pictures and used up many rolls of film before I could finally say that I was proud of my photos.

If I had to name one person who showed me anything, it would be Pierre Garnier. He sold me all the right equipment, he explained about all the chemicals and what they do. If I had to pick one person who actually taught me something, it would be him. I always made contact prints, never enlargements. As far as larger formats go, I've done some in 13 x 18. People usually didn't ask for enlargements, but when they did, I took the work to Garnier's studio. All of my enlargements were done there.

ML: ***You're particularly good at posing people in interesting ways.***

SK: I invented that myself as I went along, since more and more people were starting to come to have their picture taken. I had to find a way to make the customers happy. That's something every photographer has to figure out for himself, and that's why I had so many clients. After all, I wasn't the only photographer in Bamako. At that time there were a few others, an older guy named Youssouf Traoré and a man from Guinea who worked in Bamako-Koura. Altogether there were three of us. From the very beginning, I always saved my negatives, from the first photo to the last, all of them.

One time I was at Youssouf's studio and a woman came to have her picture taken. He did a few poses, maybe three different ones. I took the negatives home to develop them and print the pictures, and when I brought everything back to him the next day, do you know what he did? He threw away the negatives! When I asked him why, he said that there was no reason to keep them around. I told him that I kept every negative of every picture I'd ever taken, but he seemed to think that it was a waste of time and space. I pointed out, however, that if a customer ever came back to him to get a new print of a photo, he'd end up having to reshoot that older photo in order to create a second print. Whereas as far as I'm concerned the original is always better than a reproduction. Still, he wasn't interested in my idea and he threw out the negatives. "Too bad": that was his final word on the matter. I still keep my negatives, though; I always have. Of course, I also really, really like my work. Every year, when I go through them, when I check all my negatives, I say to myself, "Seydou's the one who did that." Well, that makes me very happy.

ML: *How many negatives have you saved?*

SK: Thousands, literally thousands. Particularly in 13 x 18 format. I kept them all. Whenever I look at my negatives I feel proud of the work I've done. Every year I'd go through all of them and clean the old ones. I cleaned them every single year, and nonetheless there were some that started to decompose. When I found negatives that were in a state of decomposition, I'd take them out of the collection and throw them away.

ML: *What are your thoughts about the enlargements that have been made from your negatives for recent exhibitions of your work in Europe and the United States?*

SK: You can't imagine what it was like for me the first time I saw prints of my negatives printed large-scale, no spots, clean and perfect. I knew then that my work was really, really good. The people in my photos looked so alive, almost as if they were standing right in front of me, in the flesh. I had only ever contact-printed directly from negatives. I never needed to make enlargements; the 13 x 18 format was really in vogue at the time and that was all people ever asked for. It was called the postcard format. People would come and request it specifically when they wanted to send a photo in a letter. I had a piece of cardboard and I would split the shot in two by putting a piece of cardboard over the lower half of the camera.

ML: *In order to create two images on one sheet of film?*

SK: That's right! That's how I made the postcards. Anyway, life went on like that for a while, until the day my father saw my photos. He was so pleased with my work; he couldn't believe it! The time seemed right for me to see if I could have a proper darkroom for developing photos. At that time I'd already ordered three 500-watt lights. In my career as a photographer I think I've tried just about everything. When you get used to a certain technique, you become the expert! I also know quite a bit about film speeds and exposures. I work with Kodak, even though I started out with Lumière film. I even repaired cameras, such as Super 8 [movie cameras]. They were little hand-held cameras. I took them apart and I made drawings of how they were put together. The sketches were for my own reference because if I didn't take them apart and see how they were put together, I would never be able to repair them. When I disassembled them I'd note all the different colored wires, I wrote it all down. Then, I'd put them back together. By doing all that work I was finally able to understand the kinds of technical glitches that ruin rolls of film.

ML: *I understand that you worked for the government after Mali became independent of French rule.*

SK: During decolonization, the Europeans left with all of the photocopy [photo processing?] machines and equipment; they took everything back. The state security bureau didn't have any way of creating documents for military personnel, the police, the national guard, etc. It turns out that since I'm related to the president, Modibo Keita, someone suggested that he ask me to do the job. I never really thought that they would want me to work for them. The only thing I had going for me was that I had taken lots of photos with our president before he was in office. I arrived and he told me that there was some work that they'd hired at least four different people to do and none of them could handle it. I said that I would be willing to work for them, but that I couldn't just close my studio. They explained that I could work at the bureau during the day and do my own work at night. They presented it as a sort of duty, an obligation. So I agreed, but I told them that the only way I'd consent to work for them was if I could maintain my civilian status.

By 1977 they had acquired a bunch of different machines, the most "high-tech" ones you could get at that time, and I had trained at least three people to do photography at the bureau. Around that time I had a misunderstanding with some of the military people, and I decided that I was tired of the job. They agreed to let me take retirement, and when I went home, the first thing I checked was my darkroom. I couldn't believe it. All the equipment, the cameras, the tripods, everything except the enlarger and the three projectors—which were too heavy for them to carry—had been stolen. With those few exceptions they stole everything, right down to the trashcans. I didn't know what to do; I was completely wiped out and I couldn't take pictures anymore.

ML: *What were the circumstances that led you to exhibit and publish your work abroad?*

SK: One morning while I was working on the engine for my motorcycle, three people showed up at my place. It was André Magnin with a woman named Françoise Huguier, and a guy. They told me they wanted to talk to a photographer named Seydou. Apparently they thought I was a mechanic! I tried to assure them that I was indeed Seydou the photographer, but they didn't believe me! "You're a mechanic," they kept insisting. "Forget it," I told them. "There's no use fighting about it, just come with me." I took them into the house where my boxes were kept, and I told them each to grab one and have a look at what was inside. The boxes were the kind that you usually use to store paper, but these were full of my negatives. Well, they just couldn't believe it! That's when it all began, in 1993. That's when it really started, and it just grew from there. Since then, I've been around quite a bit.

ML: ***Have you done a lot of traveling since the first exhibition?***

SK: Yes, I've traveled a lot. I've even been to New York, wow! Only very recently, I told them that I couldn't travel anymore. Whenever I go to places where the climate is cold, I end up getting sick. And then once I get back here, with the jet lag and all, things just get worse. Now Malick [Sidibé] is the one who goes to all of those things. Malick and I have really gotten to know each other. First we just knew of one another, had heard of each other's work, then we became friends.

So now you have the story of how I discovered photography and how it all began. Frankly, we work in order to earn our daily bread here. When you're the head of the household, it's your job to make sure you can feed your family! Photography started out as a means to an end for me. I never thought that there would be exhibitions.

"I'm mainly interested in capturing joyful moments, joy and pleasure. As a photographer you have to do a good job and love the work. I have friends in this line of work who say that they don't really need to love the job. Even when they take bad photos they still sell them to the client to fulfill the contract. But that's not really honest. I've taken my work seriously. For me photography has always been about the joy and the love of the work."

Malick Sidibé, Bamako, Mali, 13 November 2000

Interview by Michelle Lamunière, with the assistance of Baba Maiga
Translated from the French by Lia Brozgal

ML: *I understand that you worked in other media before you started making photographs. Would you talk about how your interest in photography developed?*

MS: I was an artist starting from my first year in school. So you see, it was kind of a natural path from drawing to photography, because both offered me the chance to create images. That's what I do with cameras, with shadows and light. You know, I really think the art of photography is in the studio work. That's where the artistry comes into play. That's when you create the scene, pose your subjects. For me, setting up a photo shoot isn't so different from drawing a scene: I decide what goes where, I decide how to pose the person in order to capture a certain physicality. It's not like taking pictures of parties, where there's a big crowd and everyone's moving according to their own rhythms, doing whatever feels right.

On the other hand, the party photography was a lot more fun. There was always music and a nice atmosphere, not a hint of sadness. Since I didn't have to worry about fixing people's hair and posing them properly, I was able to create spontaneous images of joy—and in that sense, the party pictures were more interesting for me. Also, it was the heyday of my youth. And you've got to live out those moments, especially when you're young and you haven't yet succumbed to the wisdom of adulthood, the sense of restraint that you develop, little by little, with age. These days, when I see young people dancing, I admire how well they do it, and I say to myself, "Hey, Malick—you're not so old!" Sometimes I think that youth, dancing, and joy are the only things that really matter in life. Don't you think? After that, it's all downhill. And those times were truly, truly joyful.

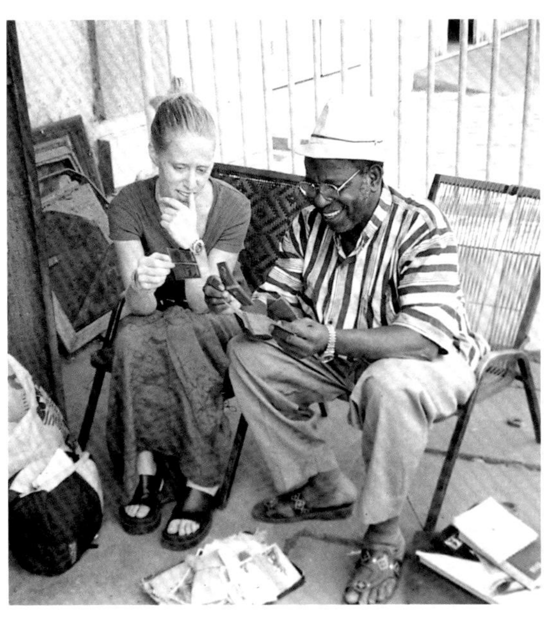

Malick Sidibé reviewing negatives with Michelle Lamunière outside his studio in Bamako, November 2000.

ML: *Did those joyful times also have to do with Mali winning its independence from France in 1960?*

MS: Yes, they did have to do with independence, but not necessarily colonial independence. There was another kind of independence, too. By 1956, Afro-Cuban music had hit Africa, along with European music, and this allowed young people to experience a different kind of freedom. Before, when things were more traditional, it was impossible for a young man and a young woman to even go near each other, let alone speak to one another. Girls weren't allowed out of the house in skirts. No way! So they wore *pagnes* [traditional wraps] over their miniskirts; that way their parents would think they were dressed properly. When they got to the party, they would take off their *pagnes* and dance. I also noticed that during that same period, girls dictated fashion for boys. If you were not hip, if you did not dress fashionably, the girls simply didn't look your way. You have to understand what a big deal it was to be able to dance with a girl: for us, touching a girl was like touching gold. At least in my youth, it just wasn't possible to touch a woman! Nowadays, boys have every chance they want. They have dance parties at clubs, usually unchaperoned. But for us, this freedom was a totally new thing, so we really got excited.

ML: ***You make it sound like a lot of fun. But it wasn't easy to make a living as a photographer, was it?***

MS: Oh, no! When I first started out, there were times when I was sleeping four or five hours a night. I needed to keep my studio open and be on time for my appointments and photo shoots. When I took orders, I would get the film one day and the prints had to be ready the very next day, at eight p.m. So I'd leave the studio around eleven p.m., head home, and process the film, first thing: develop, fix, wash, hang. At six a.m. I'd wake up and print half of the pictures—six in the morning! At seven, I'd take a shower and get over to the studio in time to open at eight. The customers would start coming, but I would still have more work to do, so I'd go back home around noon, and by two p.m. I'd be printing the other half of the pictures, so that all the photos would be ready by eight. See what I mean?

I worked like that for thirty-five years. Sometimes I'd put on music at night and I'd end up not sleeping at all. With music on, I could print until six a.m., nonstop. Can you imagine? Ha! When it comes to color, you can't really work that way. It's just not possible. Color doesn't inspire that kind of passion: anyone can snap a photo and give it to a Fotomat to develop. But there was a time when things were different, when people paid more attention to the details of photography. Back then, you only truly became a photographer once you knew how to print your own photos.

ML: ***When you started, you photographed many industrial subjects—roads, railways. How did those projects come about?***

MS: For the most part, someone would come to see me with an idea, and that is how the project would begin. It's the same with portraits, it's always up to me to work with the clients and figure out what kind of photo they want. Generally speaking, for an African photographer, getting paid is the name of the game. We don't just pick up a camera for the pure pleasure of it, you know—by and large, our work stems from an economic need. We learned it from the French. French photographers came here and set up studios, and they were able to make a living as photographers. It wasn't the love of the camera that first drew Africans to photography, it was the promise of financial gain and respectable employment. But that first taste turned into a genuine hunger, and a real passion for the art of photography was born.

ML: *Were any of your reportage photographs ever published in newspapers here?*

MS: No, not in the papers, no way! The only papers that could have published those kinds of images were the state-run papers, and they had their own photographers.

ML: *How long have you been in business as a studio photographer?*

MS: I've been in this studio since 1962. Before opening it, I took photos in other places. Sometimes I was invited into people's homes to take pictures for the family. My first job was with Gégé at Photo Service, "Gégé the film," Gérard Guillat.

ML: *Was there much competition between Gégé's Photo Service and La Croix du Sud [The Southern Cross]?*

MS: Yes!

ML: *Were these the largest photo studios in Bamako?*

MS: No, but the Photo Service was the most recent and up-to-date. That's where I worked; it was my first job. The Photo Service was an offshoot of La Croix du Sud. Gégé is actually the one who started doing news photography. It was a great success because he was well connected, and everywhere he went he took photos with various officials—at communions, at weddings. Once he made it big he started his own studio as a Photo Service. That's how it evolved. In 1956 he did a story, and I'm sorry that I don't have the negatives anymore. They were the first true photographs of Mali. He ended up leaving Mali for New Caledonia. He took photographs there for a while and apparently he had an exhibition in Paris. Once he wrote to me from New Caledonia because he'd left his studio here under the management of a number of different people. It was pretty clear that they were all amateurs. He wanted me do the studio inventory and to take over his shop. I told him I didn't think that I could handle a studio like that. So his studio just passed from one guy to another.

ML: *What are you trying to get across in your photographs?*

MS: Well, I'm mainly interested in capturing joyful moments, joy and pleasure. As a photographer you have to do a good job and love the work. I have friends in this line of work who say that they don't really need to love the job. Even when they take bad photos they still sell them to the client to fulfill the contract. But that's not really honest. I've taken my work seriously. For me, photography has always been about the joy and the love of the work.

I also like the idea of photography as a means of creating memories. People sometimes bring newborn babies to the studio, and in those cases, it's clearly a matter of creating a memory for the parents, for the mothers and fathers who want to remember their baby at that age. At the other end of the spectrum, I also have people coming in with their fathers, or their grandfathers, because they want to have an image of that person. These images are physical memories that people can keep in their family archives, for the children, for the grandchildren, for the great-grandchildren. They are the very emblem of the self. The camera functions like a mirror. It proves one's existence, or at least part of one's existence. It leaves you with a permanent trace, something that you can look at anytime you want, that you can send to friends and family. People wanted these images of themselves. It's a powerful urge that they can't always explain, or resist.

ML: *Do people still come to your studio to have their portraits made?*

MS: For the moment, I've more or less taken a break from the studio. I open up sporadically, for holidays, things like that. Since I have a studio to run, I can't afford to charge the same price as someone who works as a freelance photographer. I have overhead: taxes, rent, that sort of thing. So I really can't charge the going rate. But there are always some takers for this kind of work. Oh, that will never change. It's eternal.

ML: *There are only a handful of African photographers who are well known in the West, and two are from Mali: you and Seydou Keïta. When did you first meet him?*

MS: Actually, it's only quite recently that Seydou Keïta and I have become friendly. I always knew who he was, but I kept my distance, and we never got to know each other personally. Here in Africa, there is a strong distrust of competition. Do you know what I mean? I couldn't simply wander over and pop into his studio, just like that. I am the younger photographer, and if I started showing up at his studio and then later on his business started to flounder, or the jobs stopped coming in, he might well think, "That young guy put a spell on me!" That's what always kept me from going over to his studio. In 1952, when I first came to Bamako, Seydou was already very well known: he had cars and all kinds of things. I was the only person in town who could repair cameras, so when his equipment broke down, he came to see me. That's how our friendship began: he would drop by from time to time, when he needed chemicals or something. After he retired in 1977, he didn't really have much in the way of equipment anymore, so he would borrow things from me. These days, I don't worry at all about going over to his studio. At any rate, we didn't do the same kind of work, really. Our styles are completely different.

ML: ***Both you and Keïta take what seem to be very stylized images of women reclining. Is there a reason for that? Is there a visual tradition that you're both responding to?***

MS: Well, I think it is something that is created. The photographer can create that effect himself; however the subject—the women in the case you mention—can also create the image according to her own vision. Sometimes a woman comes to my studio and she wants her picture taken with a radio. Sometimes a woman comes looking for a more quiet, laid-back atmosphere, as if she were in her bedroom. If the photographer can sense what she wants, the end result can be very charming. There's a sort of serenity and ease, almost as if she were at home, not in a photography studio. On top of that, the photographer also has to work with clothing and fabric. The photographer can tell the woman what fabrics and clothes work best for her.

All these things add up to buying power, like jewels, or other luxury items—European goods, especially, since not everyone can afford them. A simple watch or a tie around a man's neck, these things say that he's someone with financial means, someone important. It's like when I was young, and there were kids who could afford to go to Paris—to Saint-Germain-des-Prés even! Sometimes, you could find the same clothes or the same fabrics at one of the boutiques here in Bamako, but it's always far more impressive if it comes from Paris. Kids are like that, as I'm sure you know. Especially in those days, the mere fact that it came from the West gave the wearer a certain kind of power, a kind of power that kids are looking for. Grown men, too, I suppose.

ML: ***It's fascinating to hear you talk about your portrait work, because in the West you're known primarily for your fantastic pictures of parties.***

MS: Yeah, well, André Magnin organized the exhibits and the book, and he didn't show all of my work. It was more or less just party pictures. That's fine, but I've taken so many other kinds of pictures! Listen, I understand the way things work. Seydou has a collection of portraits, and so they prefer to show my candid work, in order to have some variety. Seydou's portraits, Malick's candid photos, I see how it works.

But still, I'm really happy to have my portraits shown so that people can discover them, too. I've said that it's much more exciting to work on studio portraiture than to take candid photos or do journalistic work. In fact, I've taken more studio portraits than party shots. At my place I can photograph so many different kinds of things: shoes, watches, bracelets, shoulder bags, necklaces. That's what brings the women to my studio to have their portraits taken. They all want their photos taken with those things.

BM: They want to show off their new braids!

MS: Right, the braids: every time the braids change, they want to have new photos taken. Every time there is a new fashion in dresses, they come to get their picture taken. Every time they get new shoes—everything! For women, particularly in an era when the media are everywhere, fashion is a very strong force. There's a new style in Europe, and some Africans go there on vacation—barely a month passes, and the style has hit Africa. And then there's cinema, fashion magazines, all that. A clever photographer—particularly a studio photographer—can use these things to his advantage. Nowadays, even babies have to be well dressed. Don't get me wrong: a well-dressed baby is really nice. But you know how it is with children. It's the mothers who dress them up like dolls. For an African woman, a baby is also a doll. She has to dress the baby well, keep him looking clean, and make sure to get photos so that she can keep the memories. You'll see portraits of kids with impressive necklaces, dressed up like adults. And it's not as if these mothers neglect their own appearance. Sometimes I even get women who show up for their portrait with perfume! They come with makeup, powder their noses to make themselves prettier, and then spray perfume.

BM: Perfume makes you more beautiful!

MS: Ha—that's it! That's how much Africans love photography. It's like religion.

ML: *Are your photographs still circulated in Bamako? Do people know who you are?*

MS: Oh yes, definitely. Sometimes women from the countryside come to have me photograph them. They know who I am, and they know I'll take a picture they really like. One woman showed up here one time, and I heard her saying, "Malick, Malick!" I turned around, but she wasn't talking to me—she was talking to her son. Not only did she know my name, but she had named her son after me! I was shocked.

You have to remember a good photographer is also a social animal. Do good work, and people love you. It's true, people love you. Because the customers don't really see the camera, they see you, the artist—you become the product they're buying. It's like sugar cubes in coffee: you stir the sugar into the coffee and it dissolves and enhances the taste. For them, the photographer has the power to make them more beautiful—that's your role. So a good photographer gets to know everyone, people of many different generations. The other day, this one kid was walking by my shop, and he called out my name: "Malick, Malick!" His friends poked fun at him, but I shouted back: "Hey, I know you!" For him, knowing me is ... well, it's really a neat thing for that kid. It's a source of pride.

ML: ***Have you had apprentices?***

MS: Yes, I like training very much. But once you've trained people they want to set up shop on their own and follow their artistic vision. Most of the people I've trained have been cousins. My first apprentice was a distant nephew. Our families were not from the same area. His father was disturbed at the idea that I'd be earning money but that his son would be working for free. He was right, what can I say? So he set up a studio for his son, which became quite a success. To top it off, since, unlike me, he had not acquired much debt, he was able to buy a car before I could afford one! Other former apprentices started their own studios here and there after I helped them set up shop. When it comes to dealing with money, people just don't get along. Some see you earning well, but they do not see your expenditures. It's tough to earn a living and pay your debts. I prefer to work with kids who are passionate about the artistry of this job because taking pictures in order to make a living is certainly possible, but it isn't fun. You've got to love what you do. The best solution for the apprentices, once they've grown up, is for them to open their own studios and make their own way in the business. That's what I did.

ML: ***I've heard you're doing a lot of work with young people these days.***

MS: Yeah, I'm working on this project using camera obscuras [pinhole cameras]—it's a very simple technique, a means of transferring an image onto a page without using a negative. We got some funding from a French organization called Obscura de France, and right now I'm looking for some more funds. In the meantime, we're still working on it, and we're still taking "obscura" photos. I'm working with young kids from the neighborhood, some of whom have never taken photos before. It's a new experience for the instructors, too, because most of us have never worked with these kinds of cameras. Even for me: I've spent lots of time repairing cameras, but I had no idea you could create an image with a simple little thing like that. Wow! That discovery was truly astonishing.

We've taken the name "Naye-Naye," which is Dogon for "light." It's great for children, even the ones who live in the bush or on the prairies, because anyone can do it, and you end up with fantastic images. I have two instructors working with me to train the kids. And there's a coordinator, a guy who is responsible for finding clients: kids who aren't working, kids who are in school, even handicapped kids.

ML: ***What about your own work? I hear you've been traveling quite a bit.***

MS: Well, not long ago, a collector invited me to Munich. She comes to Mali regularly, and every time she's here we take trips together, because she likes to photograph. She found a studio for me in Munich, and I did some work there; that was a very, very happy time. One night she and her husband were supposed to go to a concert, and they actually missed the show because they were so fascinated watching me work, seeing how I make portraits. I did the same thing in Geneva; I took some really lovely pictures there: young people, old people. I also took pictures in Nantes. And just the other day, I got a phone call asking if I could go to Amsterdam to shoot some portraits. It used to be that there were always twenty or thirty people around my studio in Bamako, waiting to have their portraits taken; today, it's not like that anymore. So when I get the chance to go other places and take photos, I'm happy. It keeps me young.

Plates

Catalogue numbers 1 through 14, 73, and 74 appear as figures in the preceding essay. Numbers 15 through 28 represent untitled commercial work printed by Malick Sidibé in his Bamako studio between 1962 and about 1980. Numbers 29 through 72 reproduce modern prints made for exhibition purposes by Philippe Salaün in Paris from original negatives by Sidibé and Seydou Keïta.

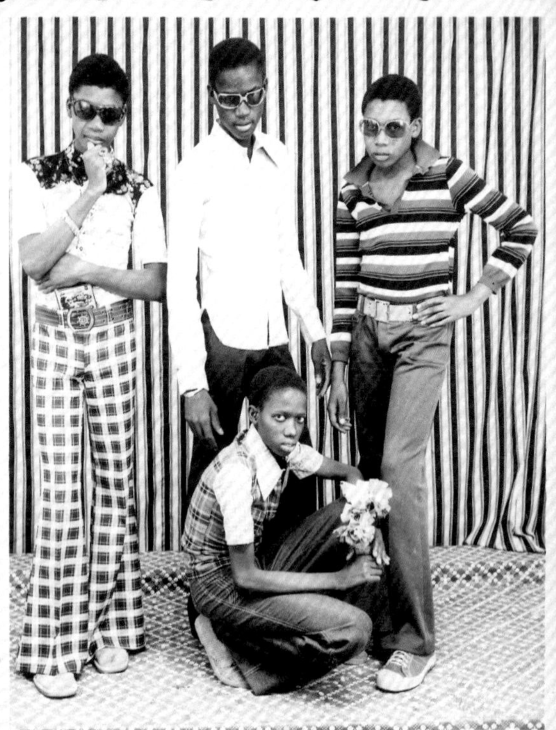

15

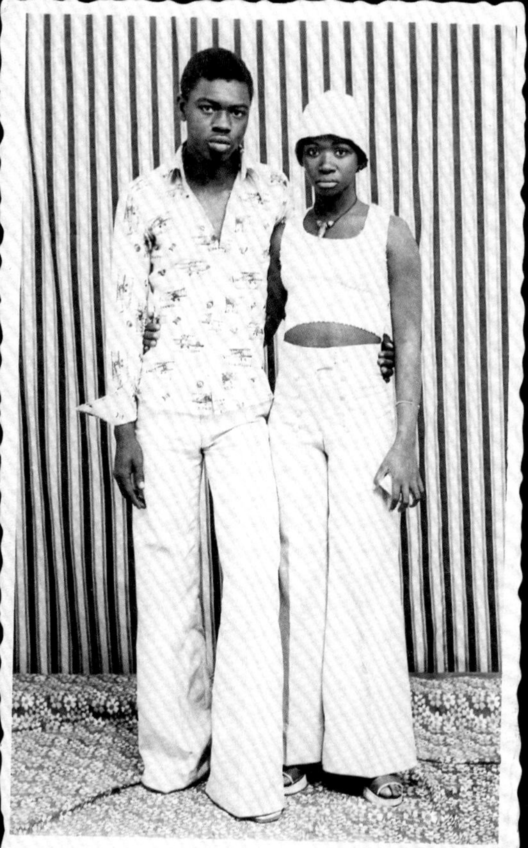

16

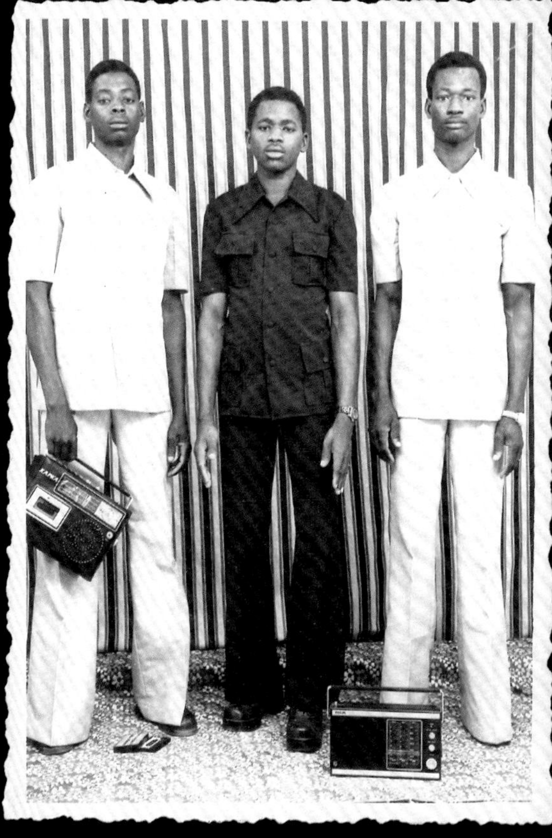

17

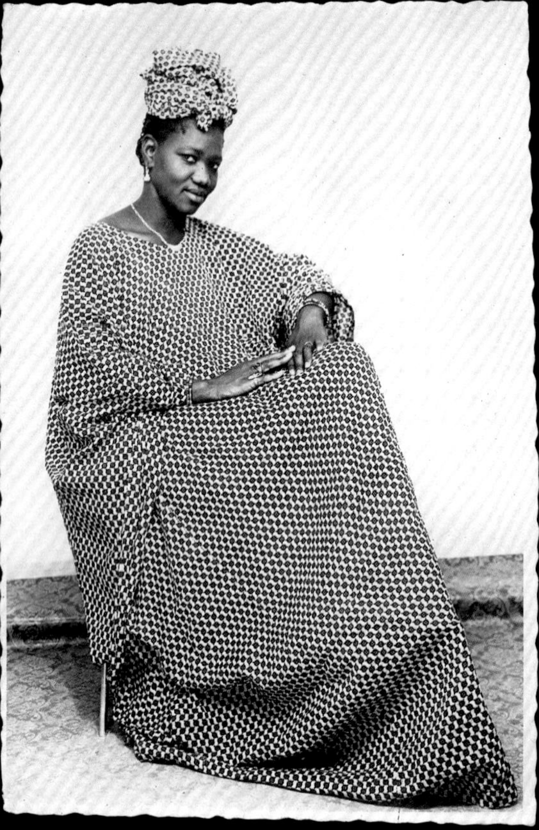

18

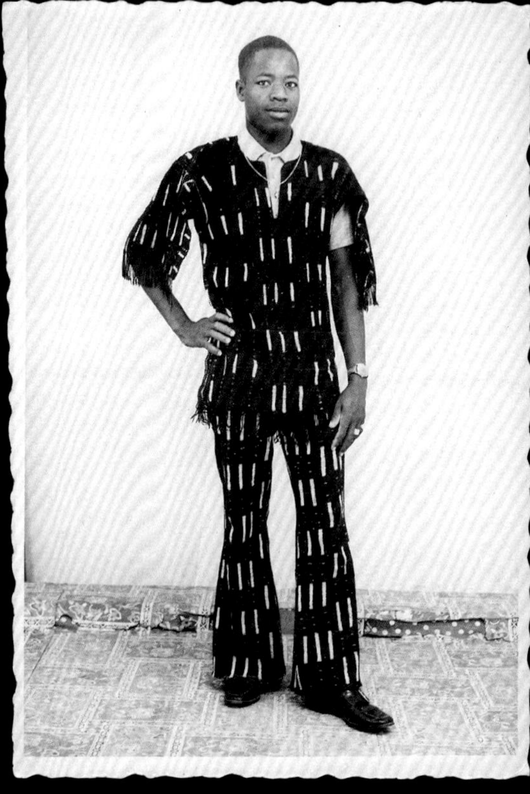

19

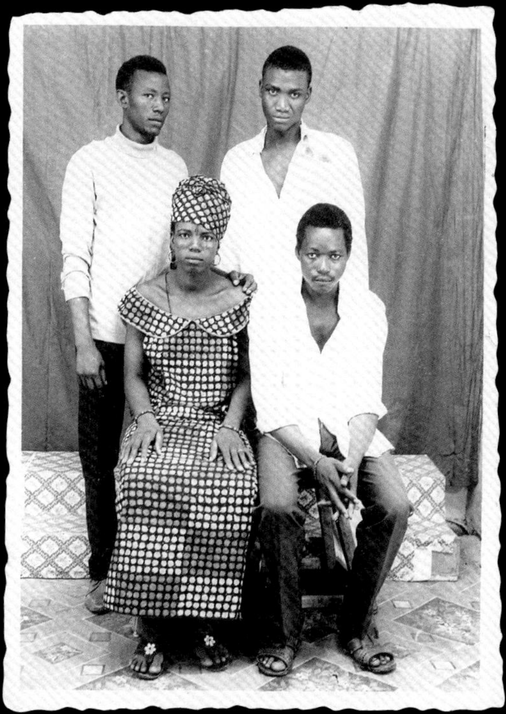

20

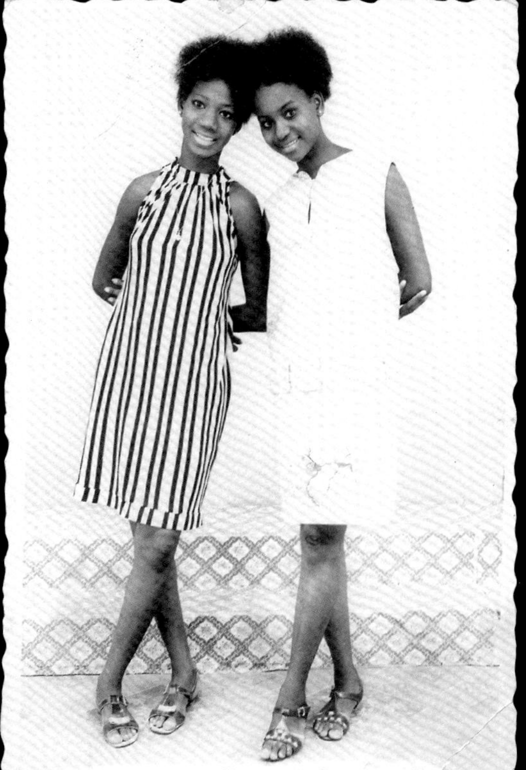

22

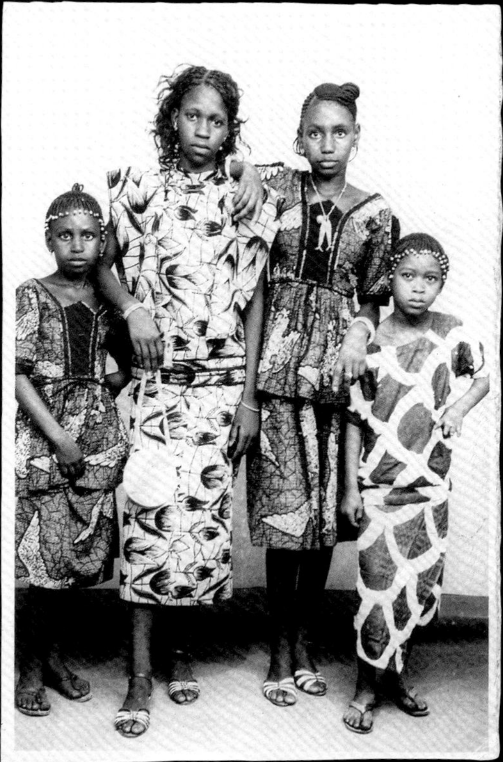

21

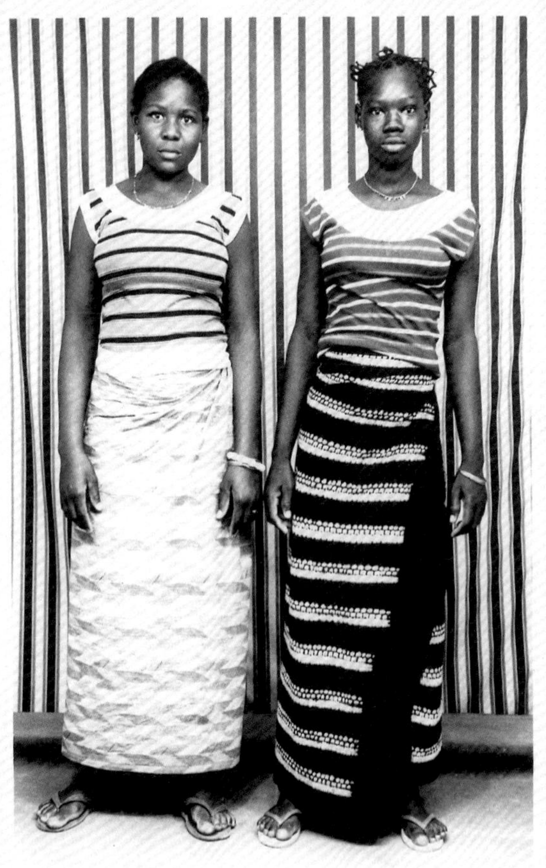

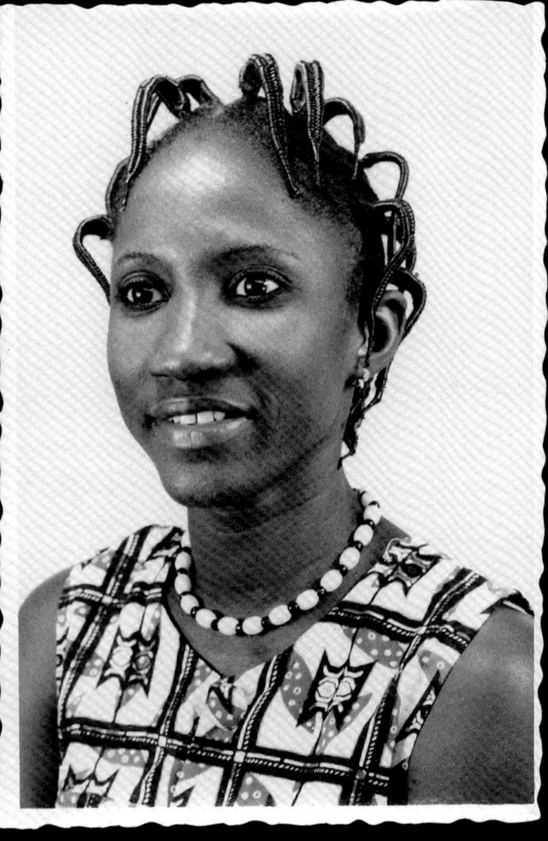

24

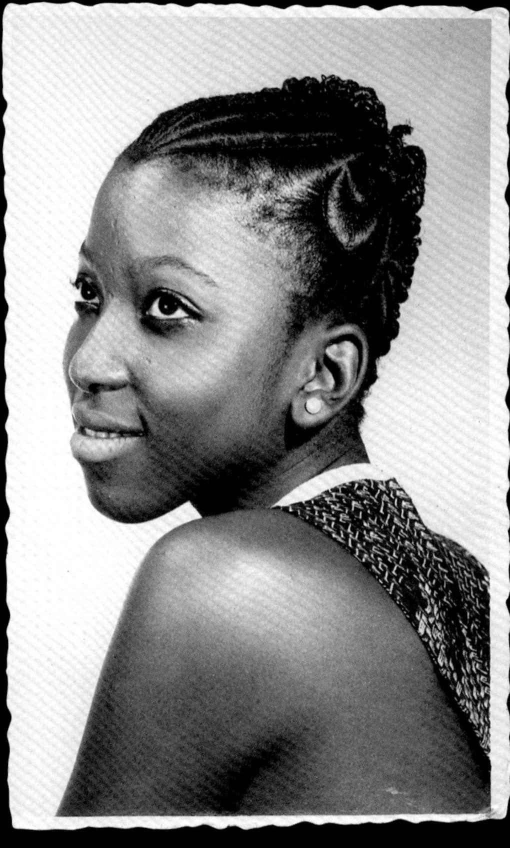

25

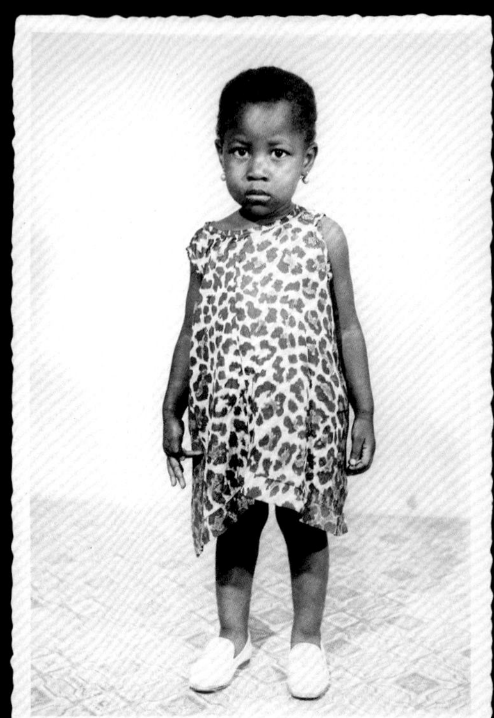

27

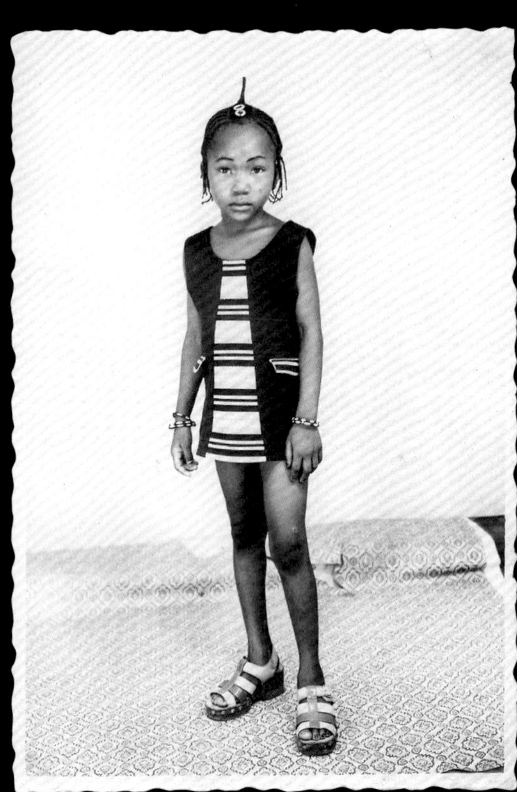

26

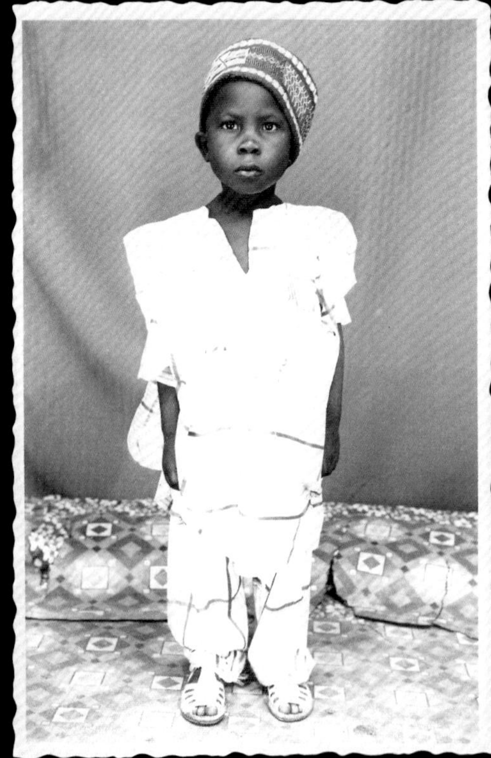

28

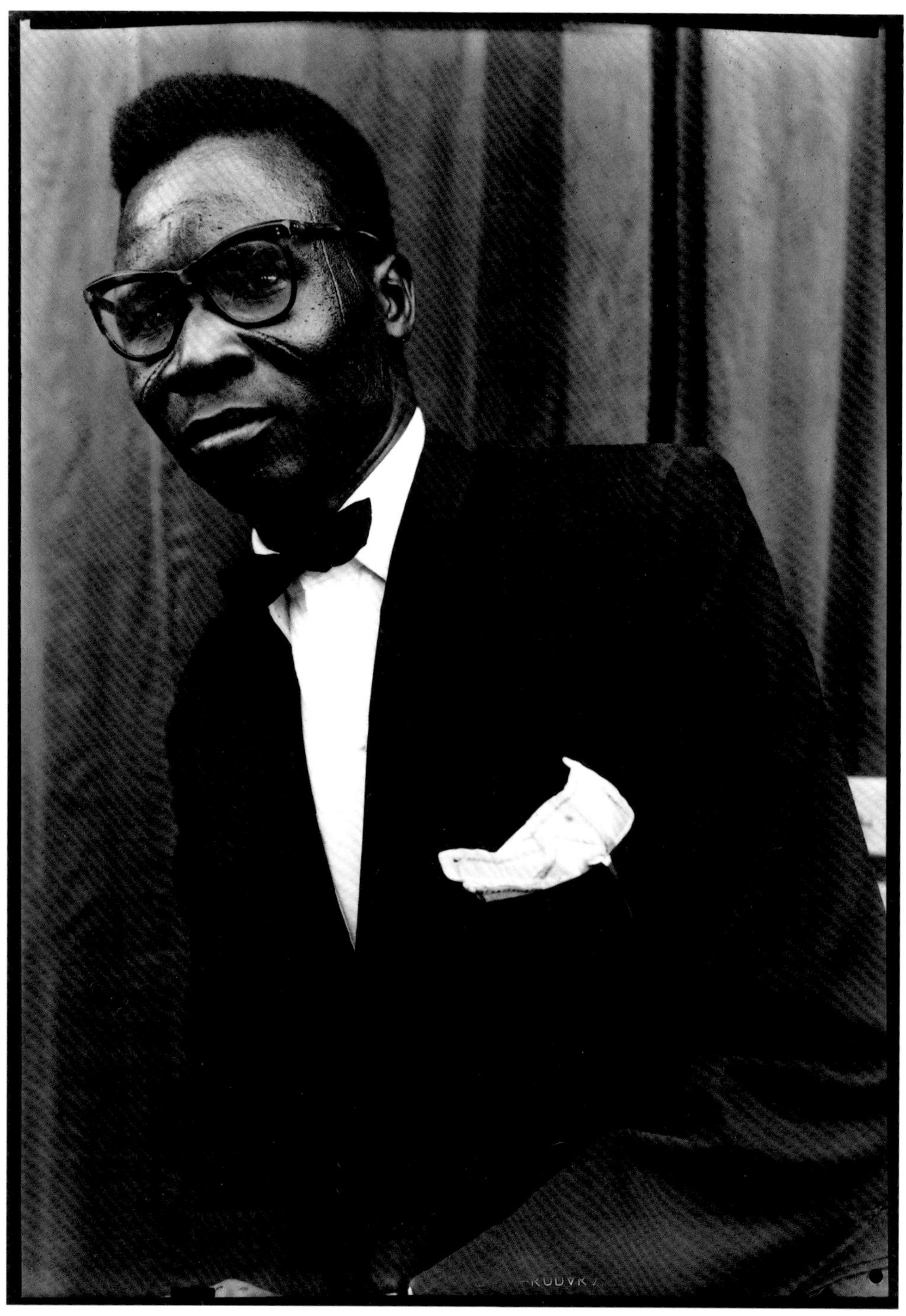

29 Seydou Keïta, *Untitled*, 1952–55

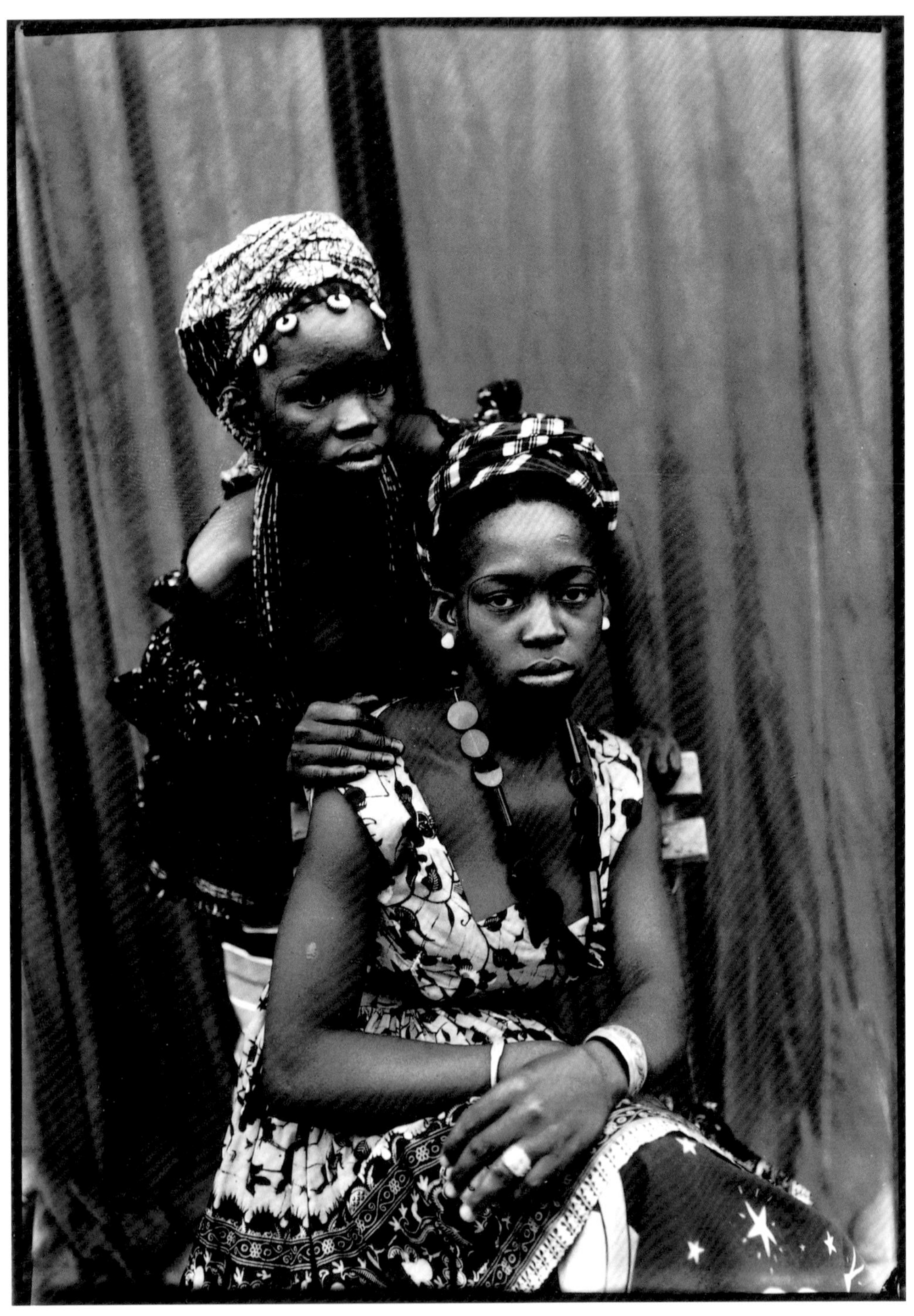

30 Seydou Keïta, *Untitled*, 1952–55

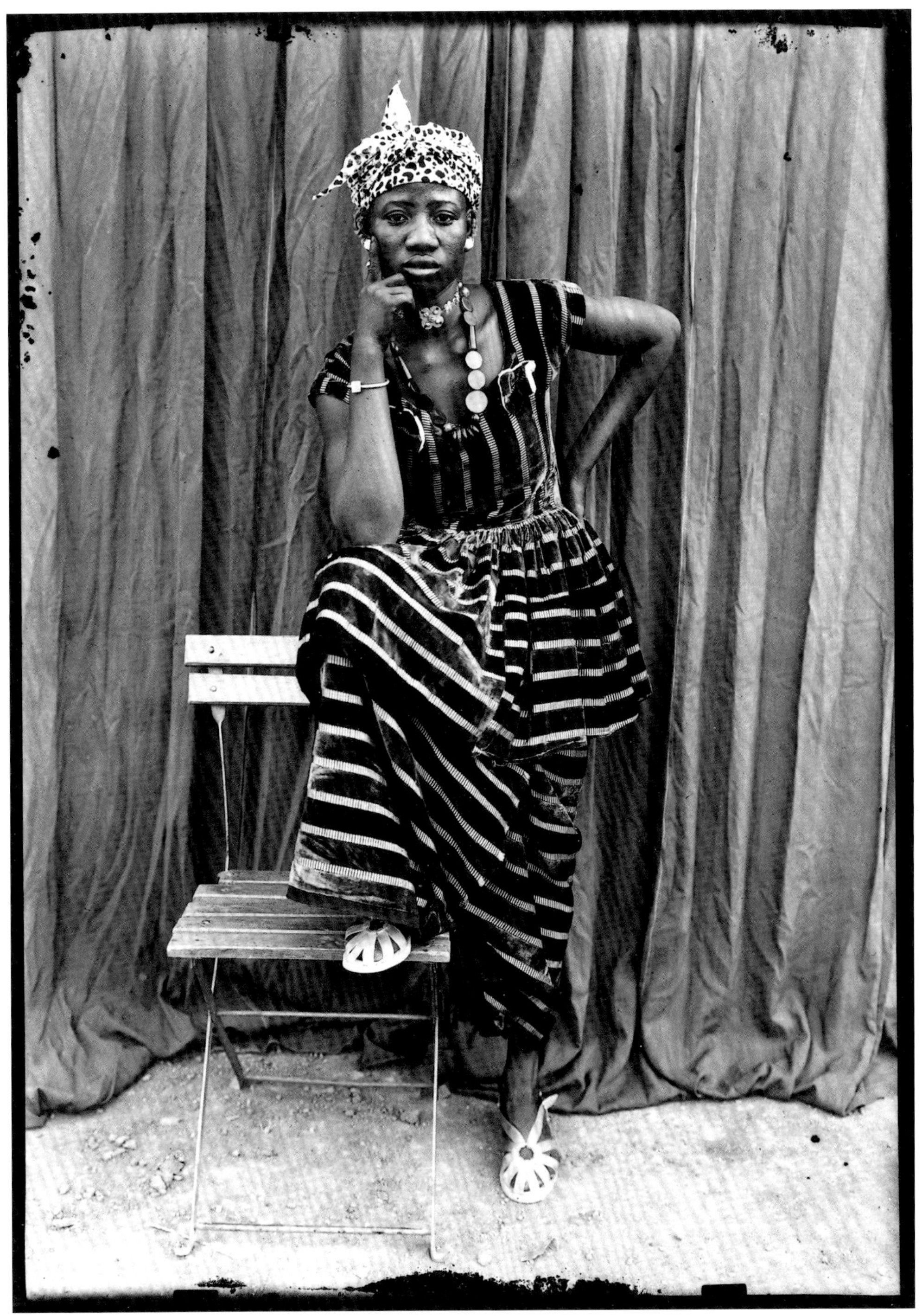

31 Seydou Keïta, *Untitled*, 1952–55

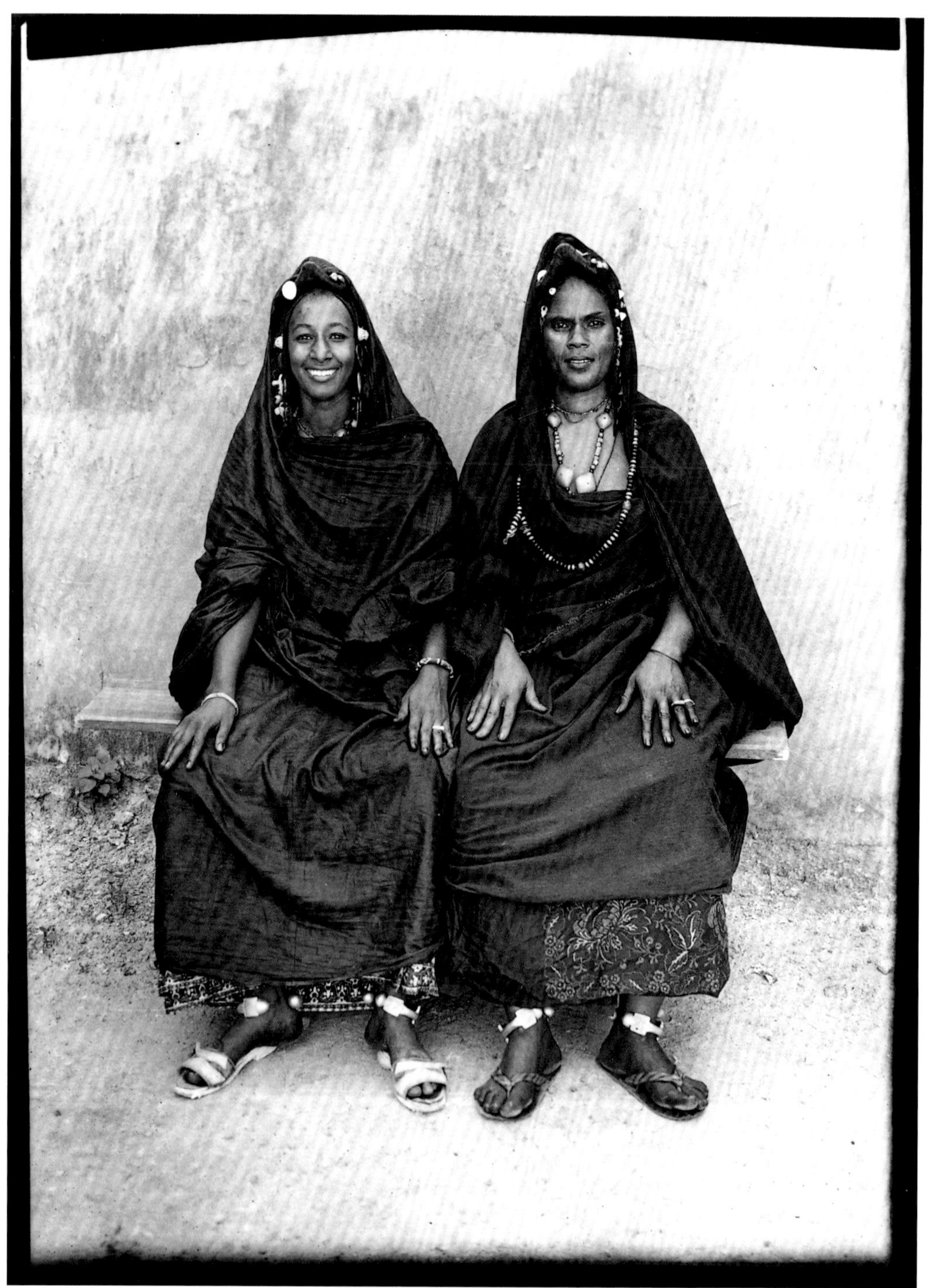

32 Seydou Keïta, *Untitled*, 1950

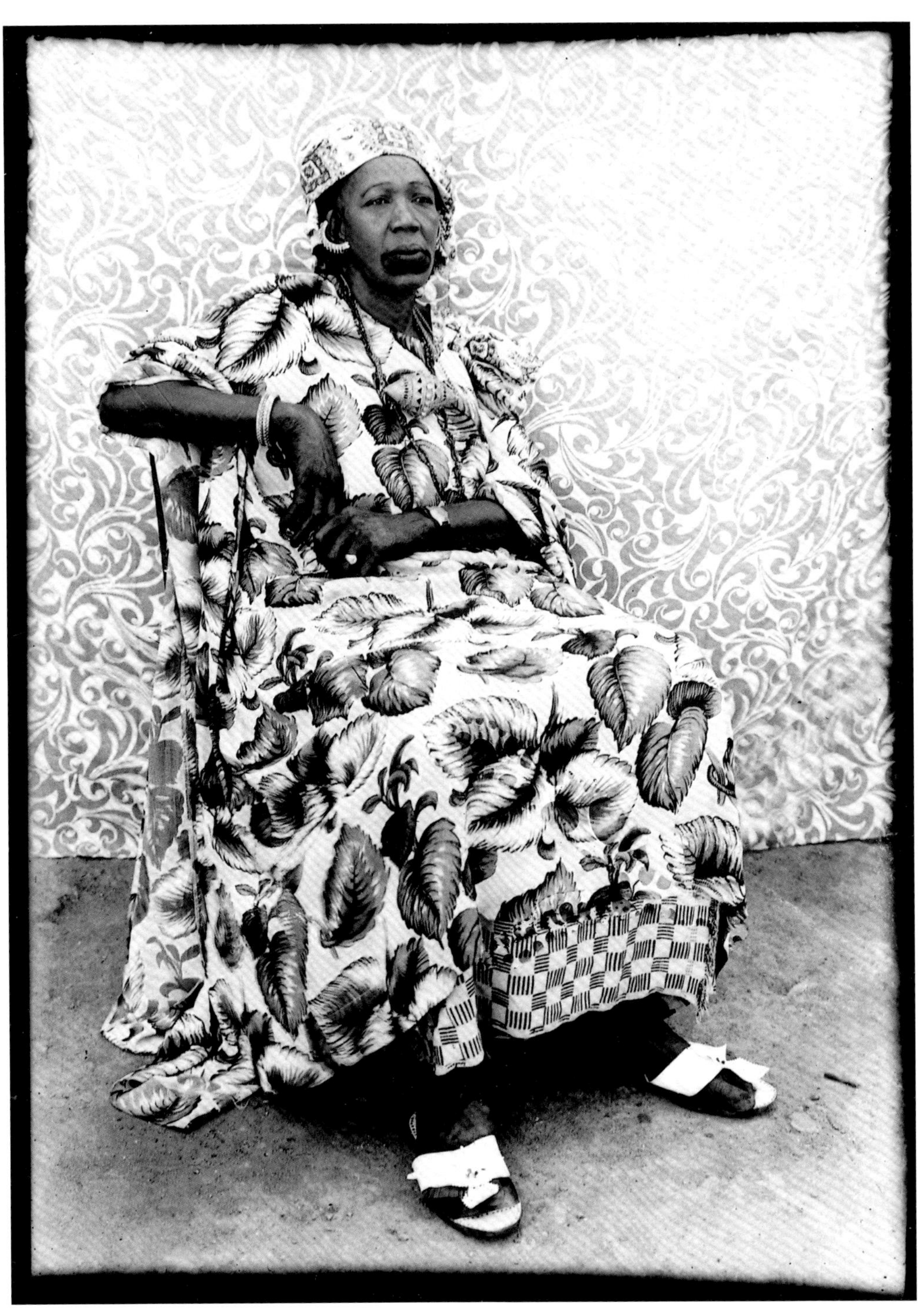

33 Seydou Keïta, *Untitled*, 1956

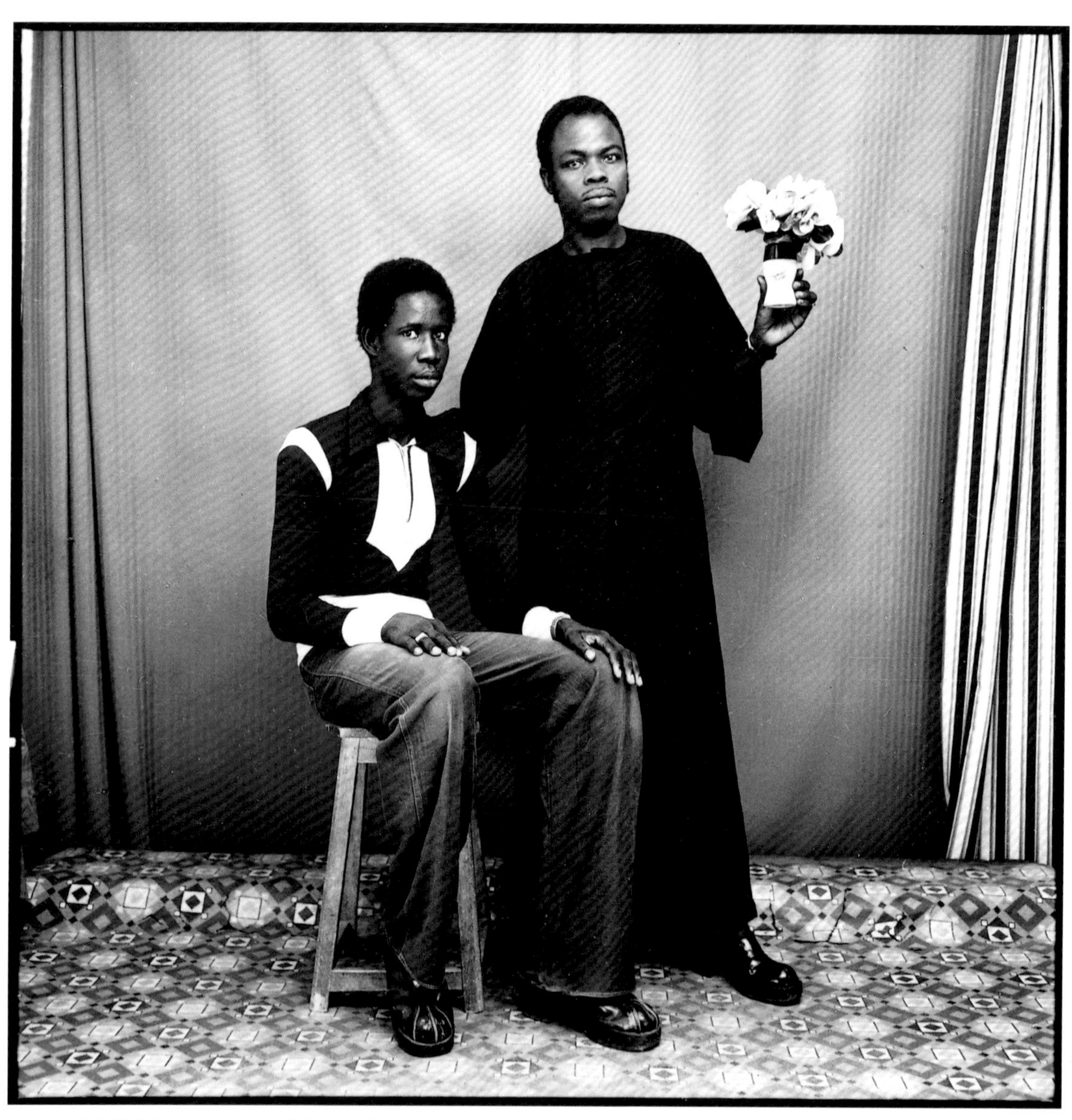

34 Malick Sidibé, *Les deux amis* [The two friends], 1975

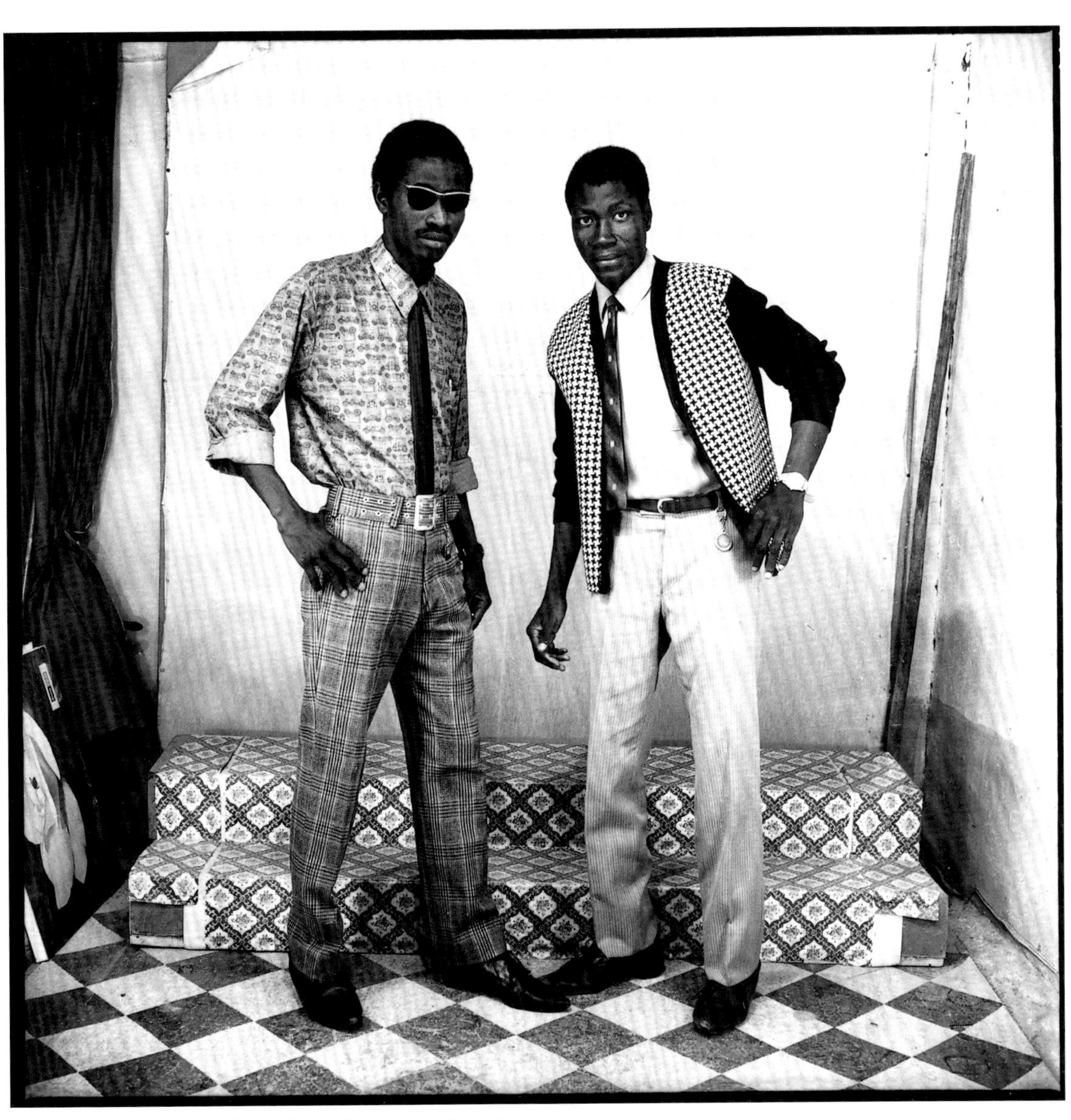

35 Malick Sidibé, *Au studio Malick* [At Studio Malick], 1969

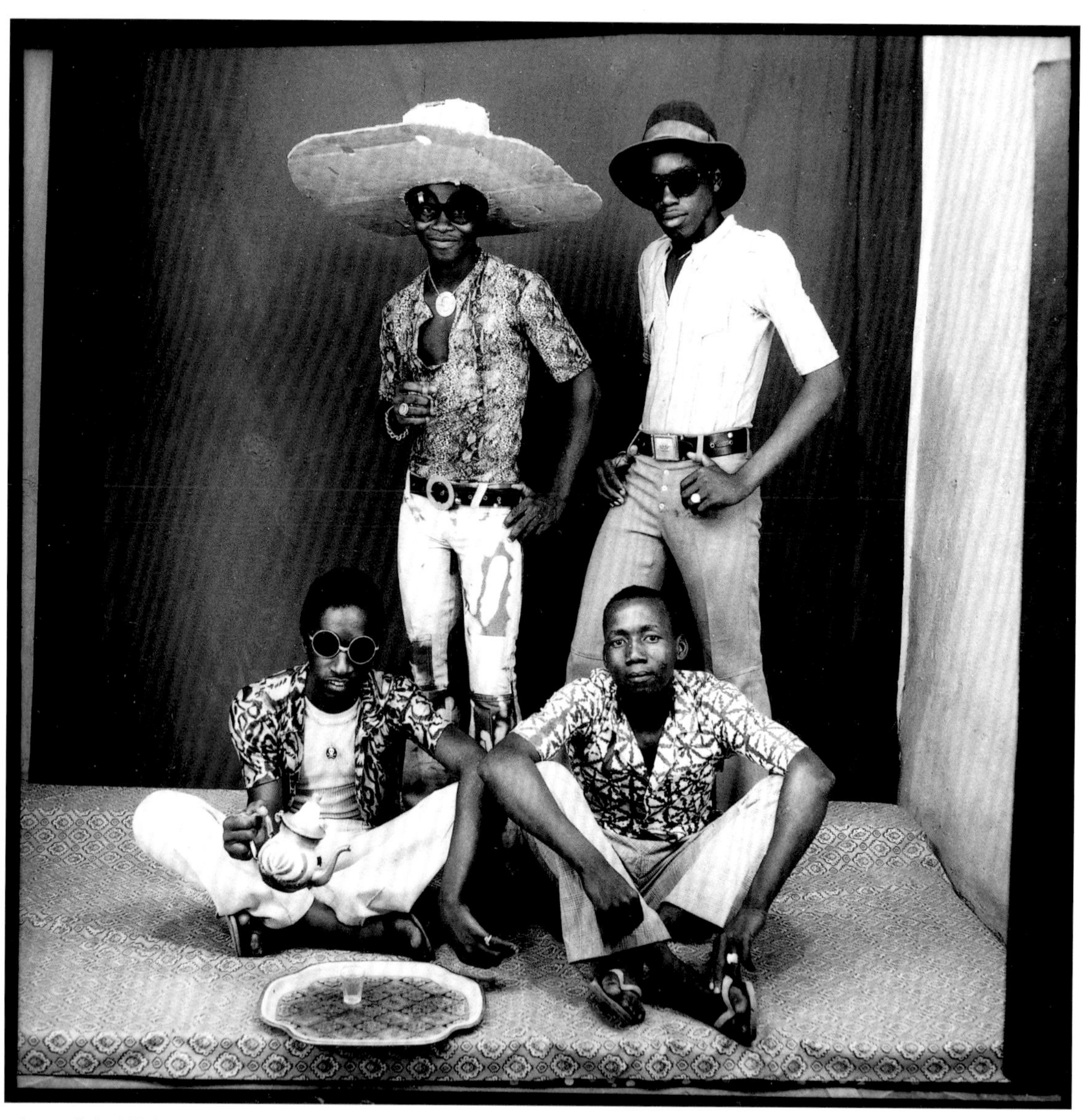

36 Malick Sidibé, *Amis des espagnoles* [Friends of the Spanish], 1968

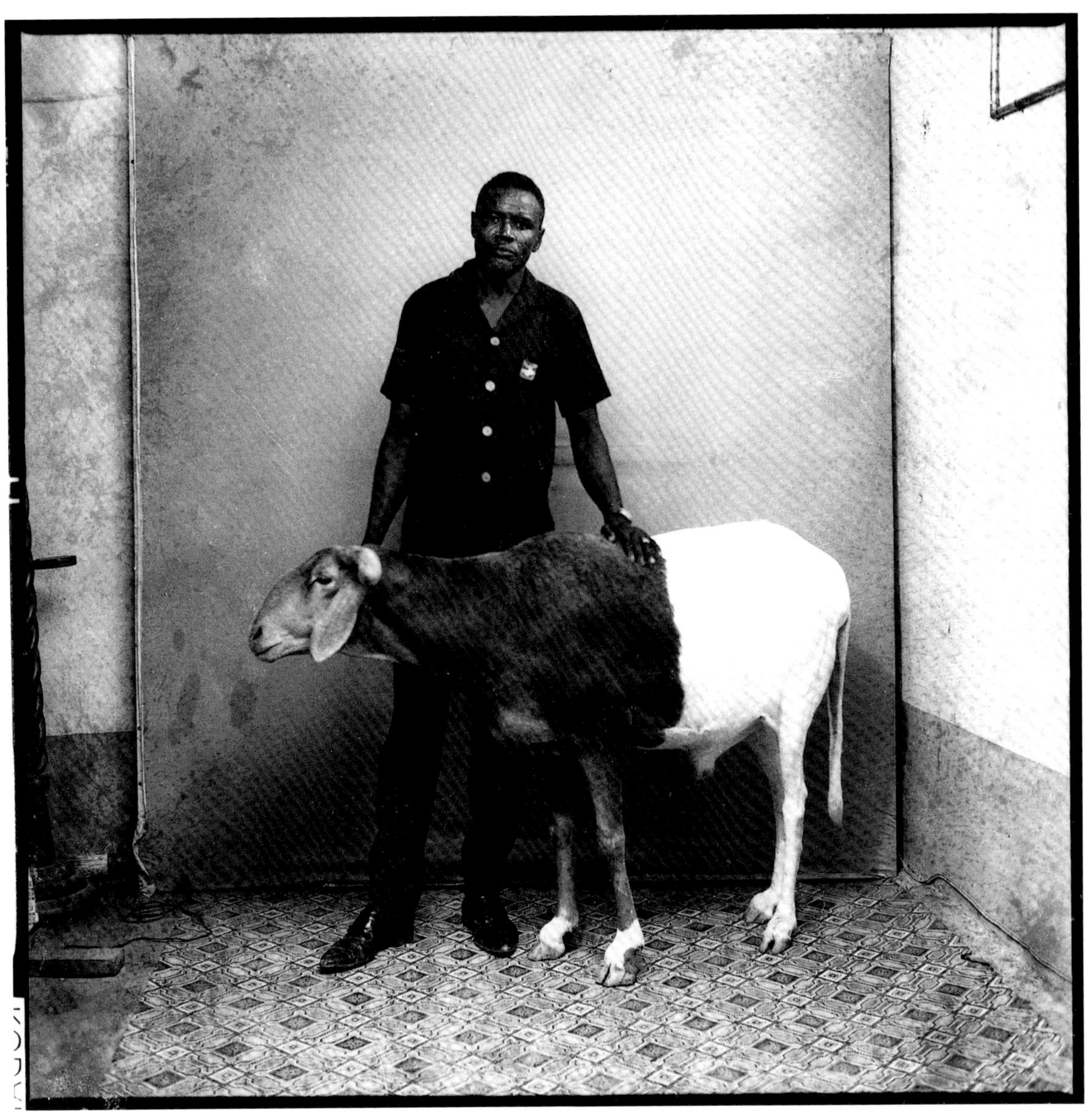

37 Malick Sidibé, *Tauré avec un mouton* [Tauré with a sheep], 1962

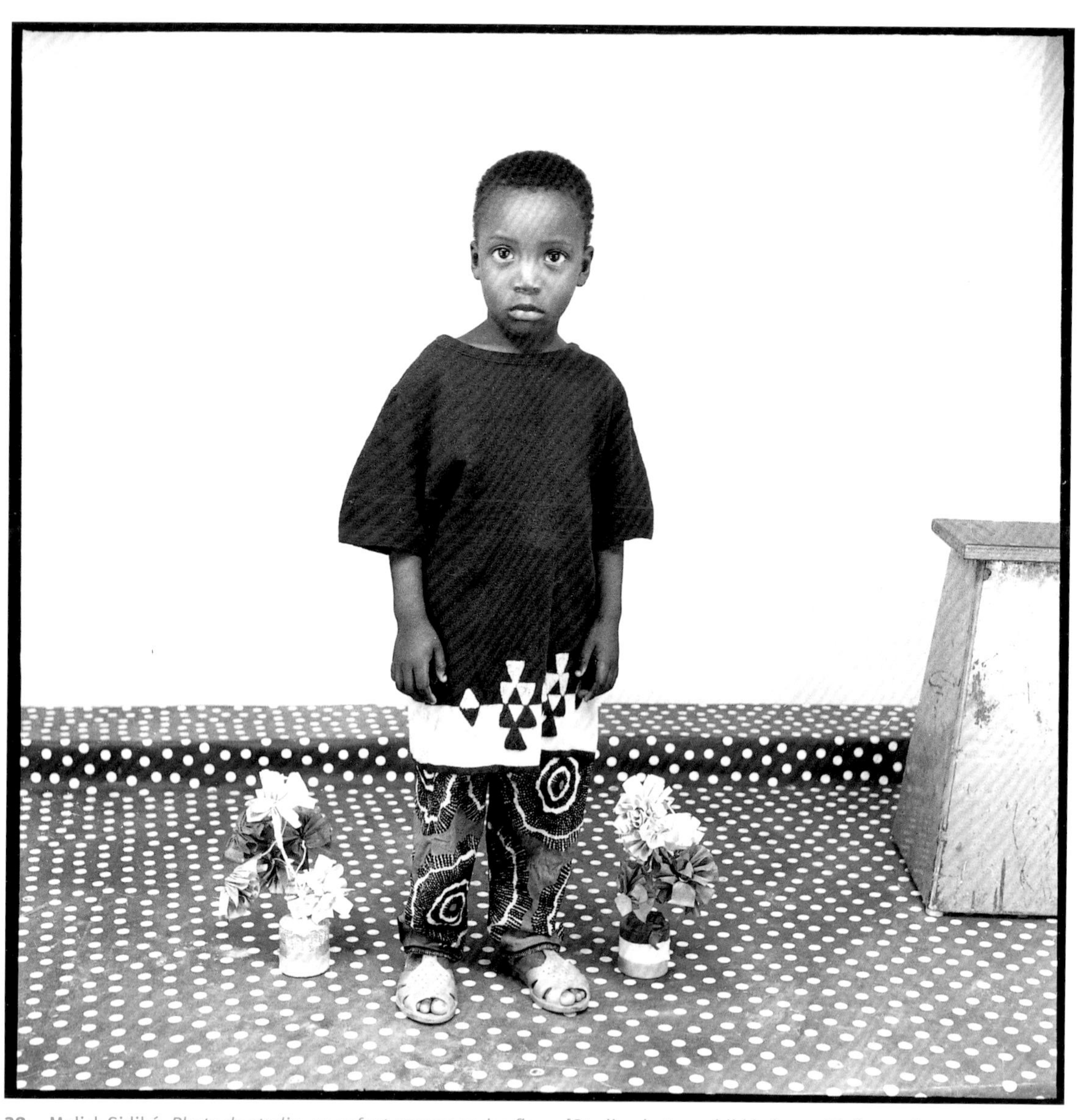

38 Malick Sidibé, *Photo de studio, un enfant amoureux des fleurs* [Studio photo, a child in love with flowers], 1975

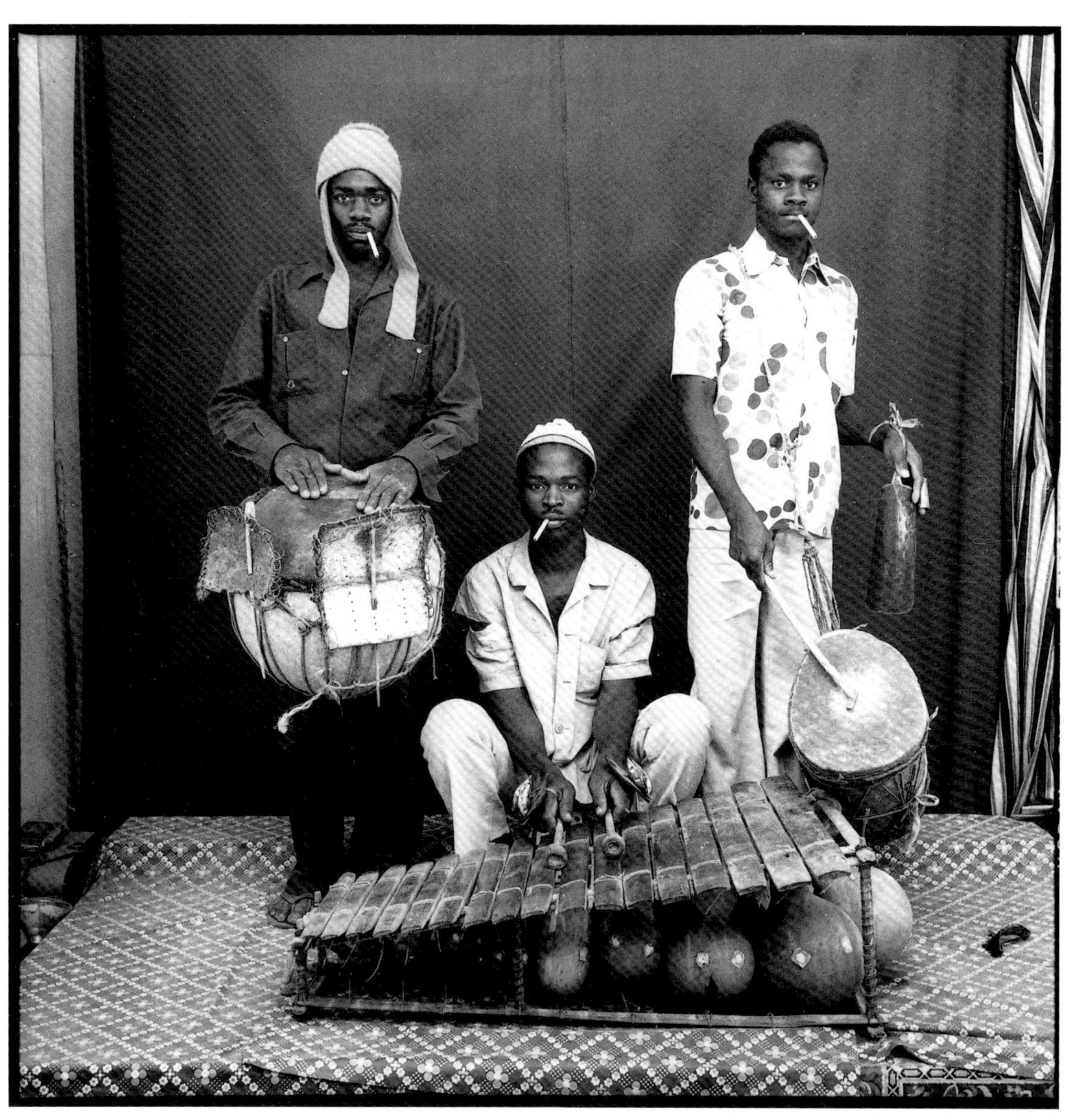

39 Malick Sidibé, *Studio musique traditionelle du Mali Balafon* [Studio, traditional balaphon music of Mali], 1975

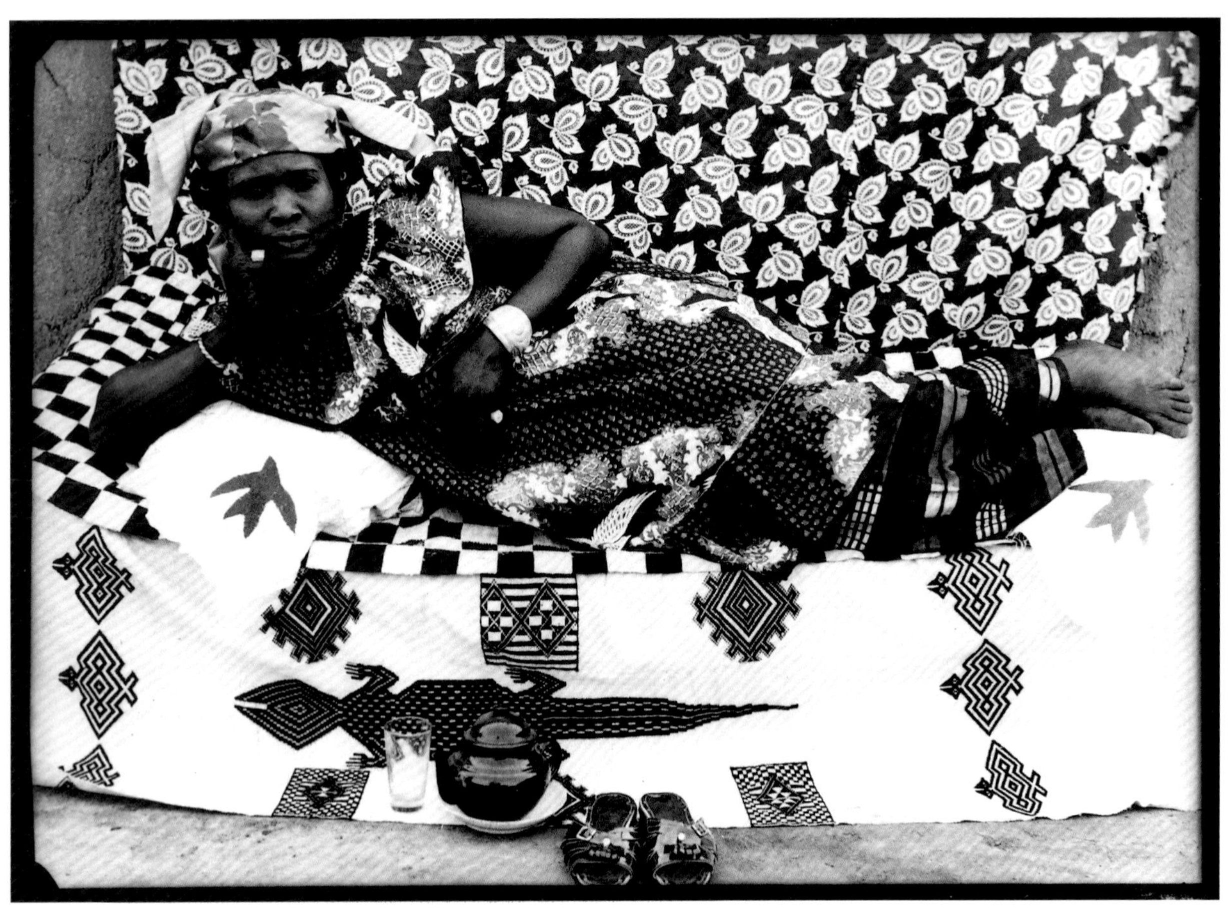

40 Seydou Keïta, *Untitled*, 1959

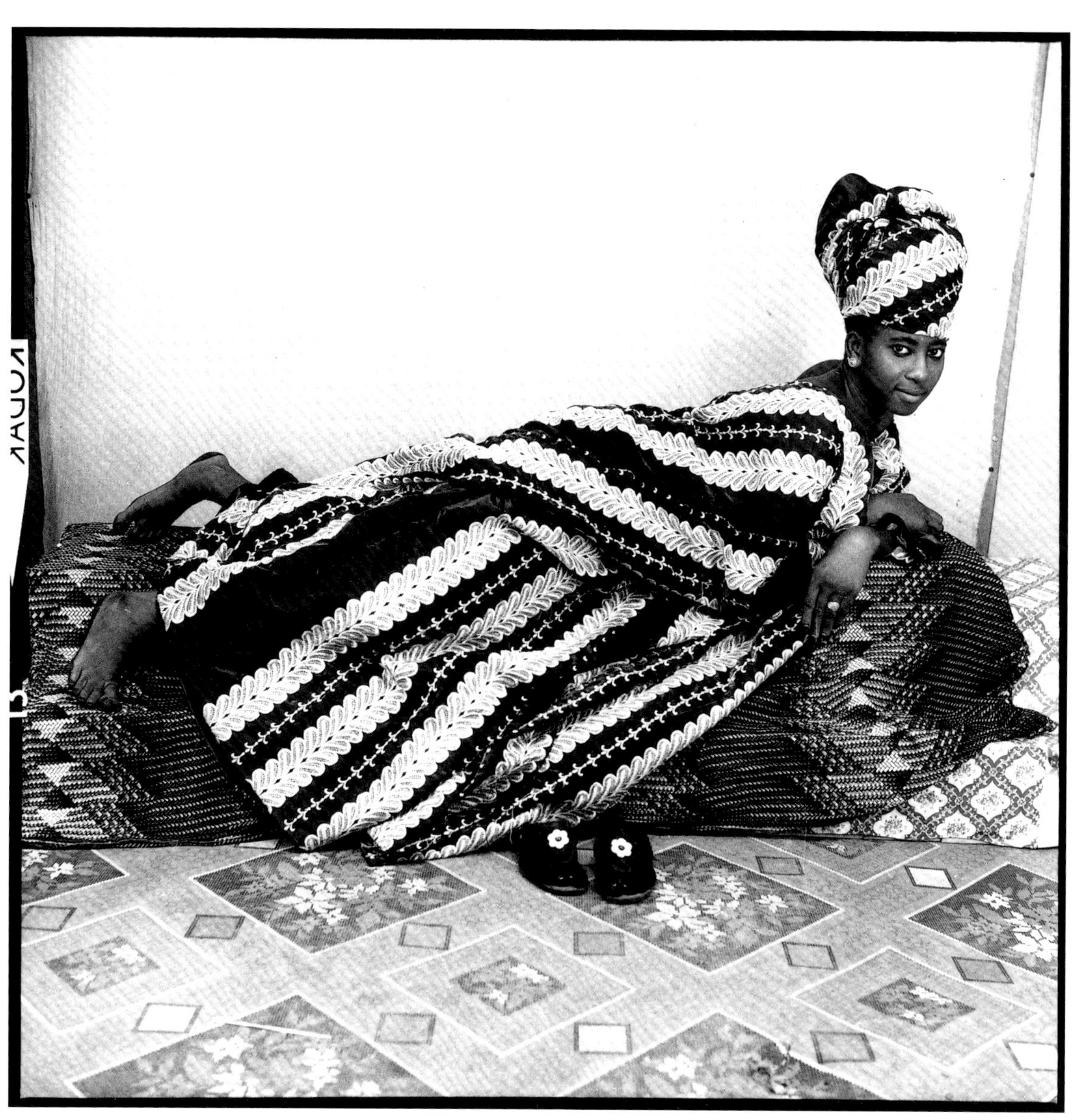

41 Malick Sidibé, *Portrait* [Portrait], 1969

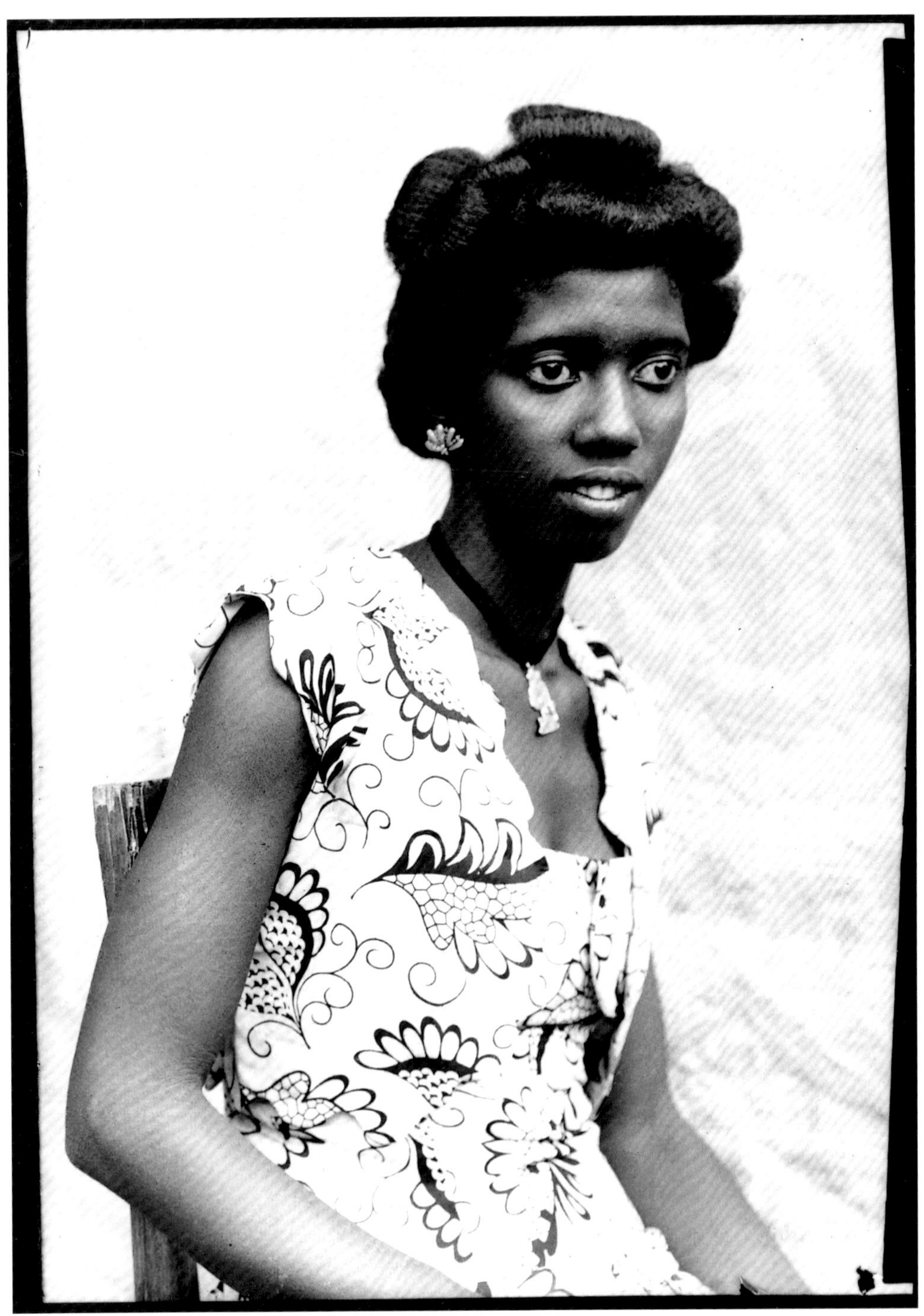

42 Seydou Keïta, *Untitled*, 1949–51

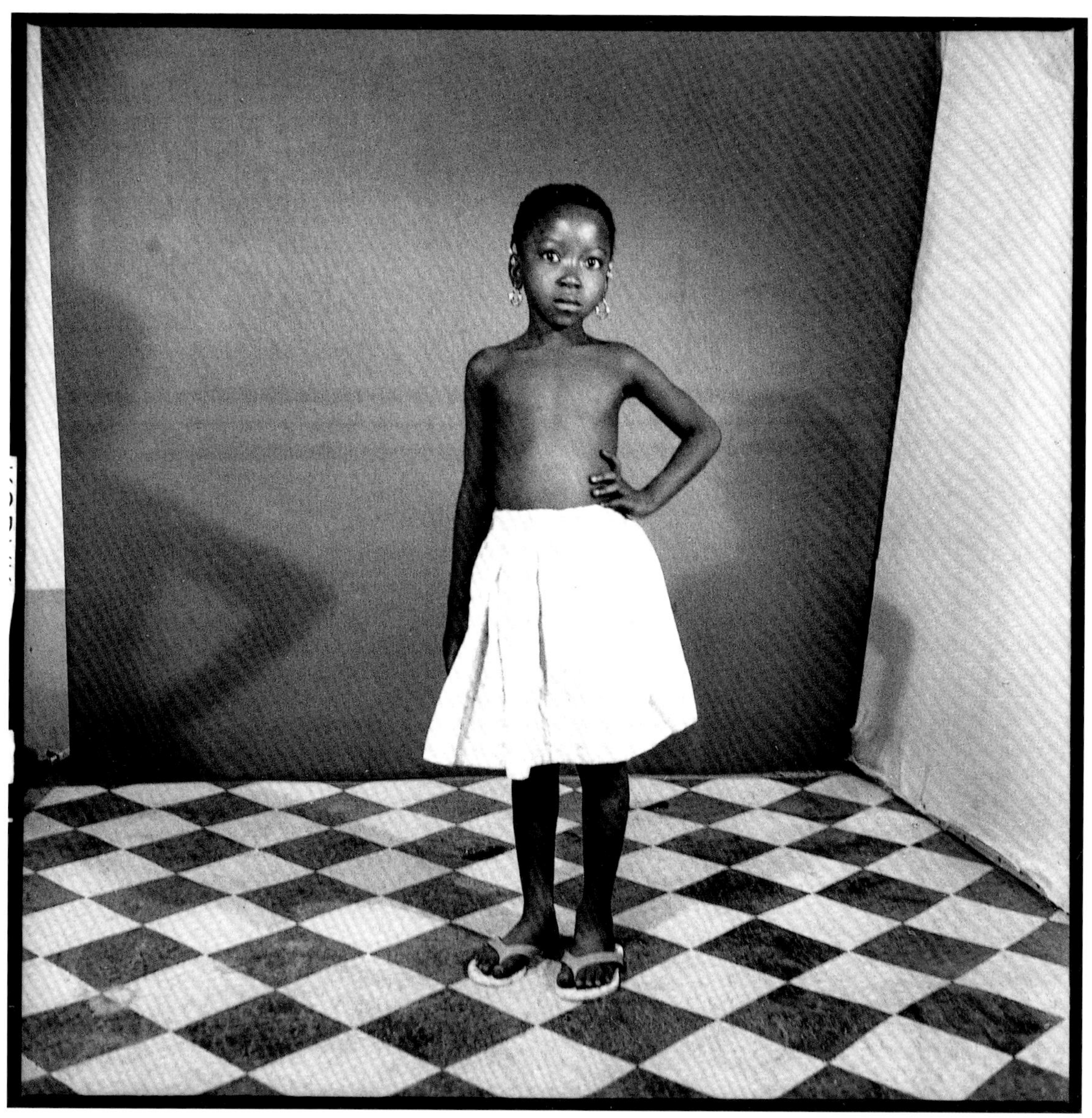

43 Malick Sidibé, *Je voudrais bien voir ma jupe* [I would like to see my skirt], 1963

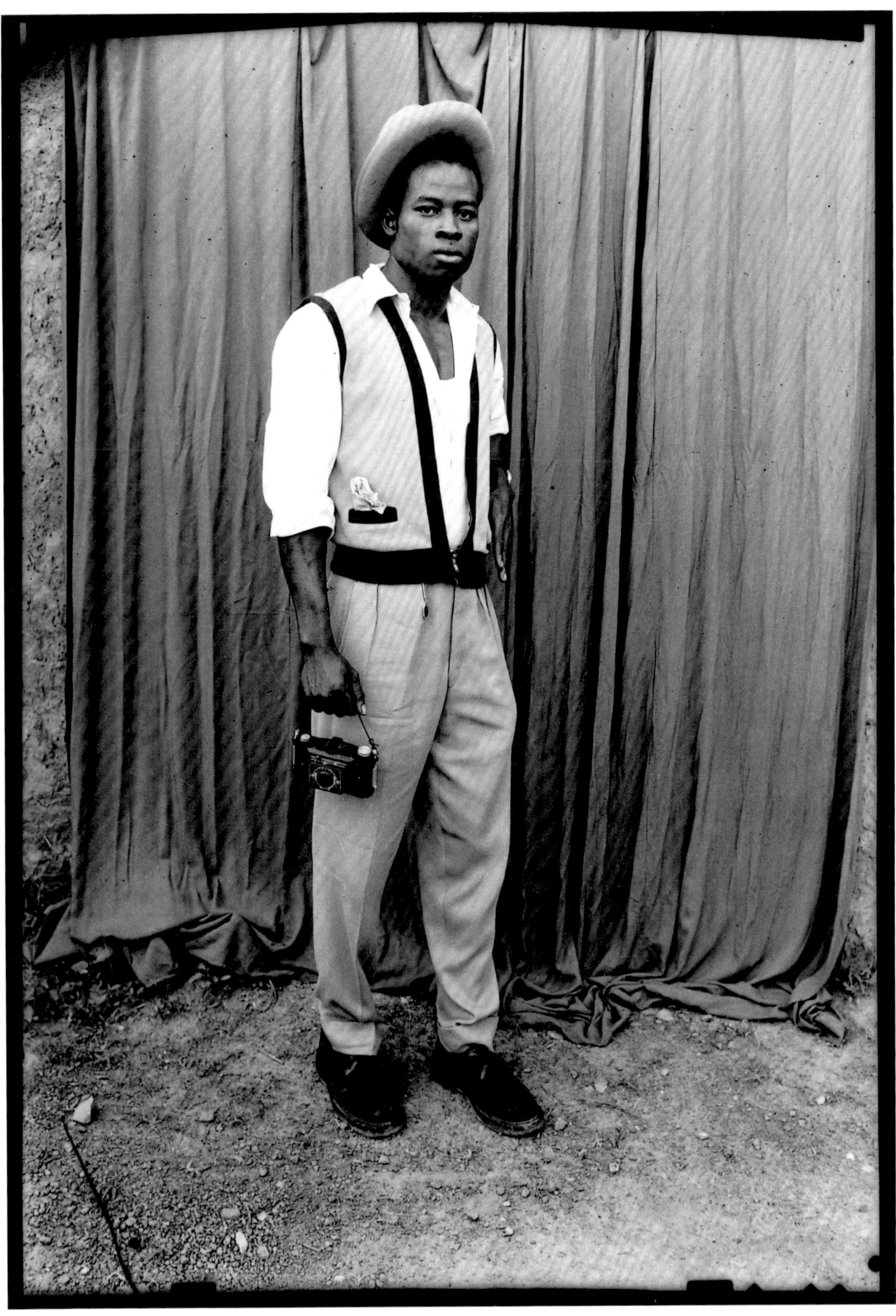

44 Seydou Keïta, *Untitled*, 1952–55

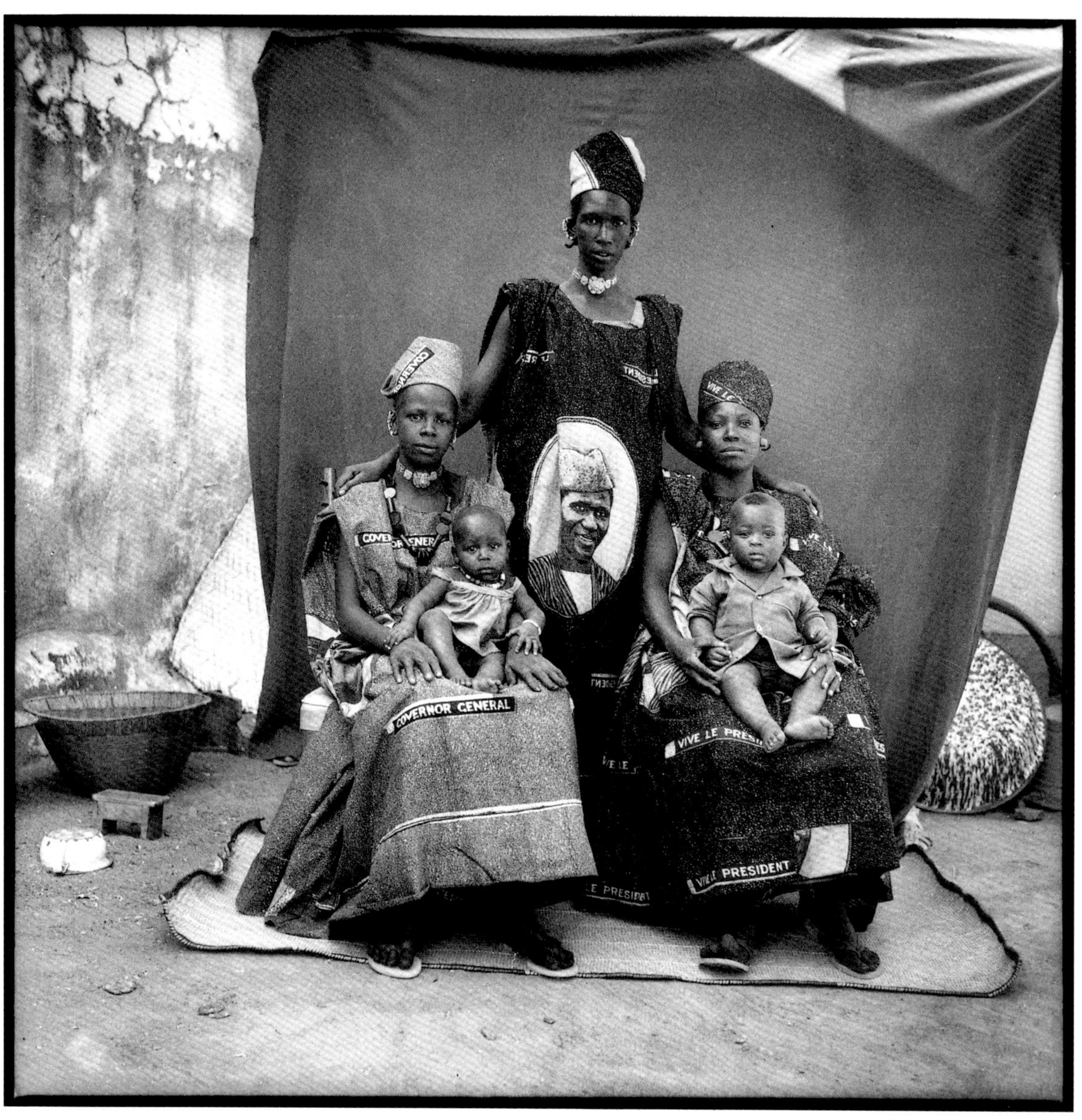

45 Malick Sidibé, *Prise de vue dans une famille Sarakolé à Mission Bamako* [Shot of a Sarakolé family at Mission Bamako], 1962

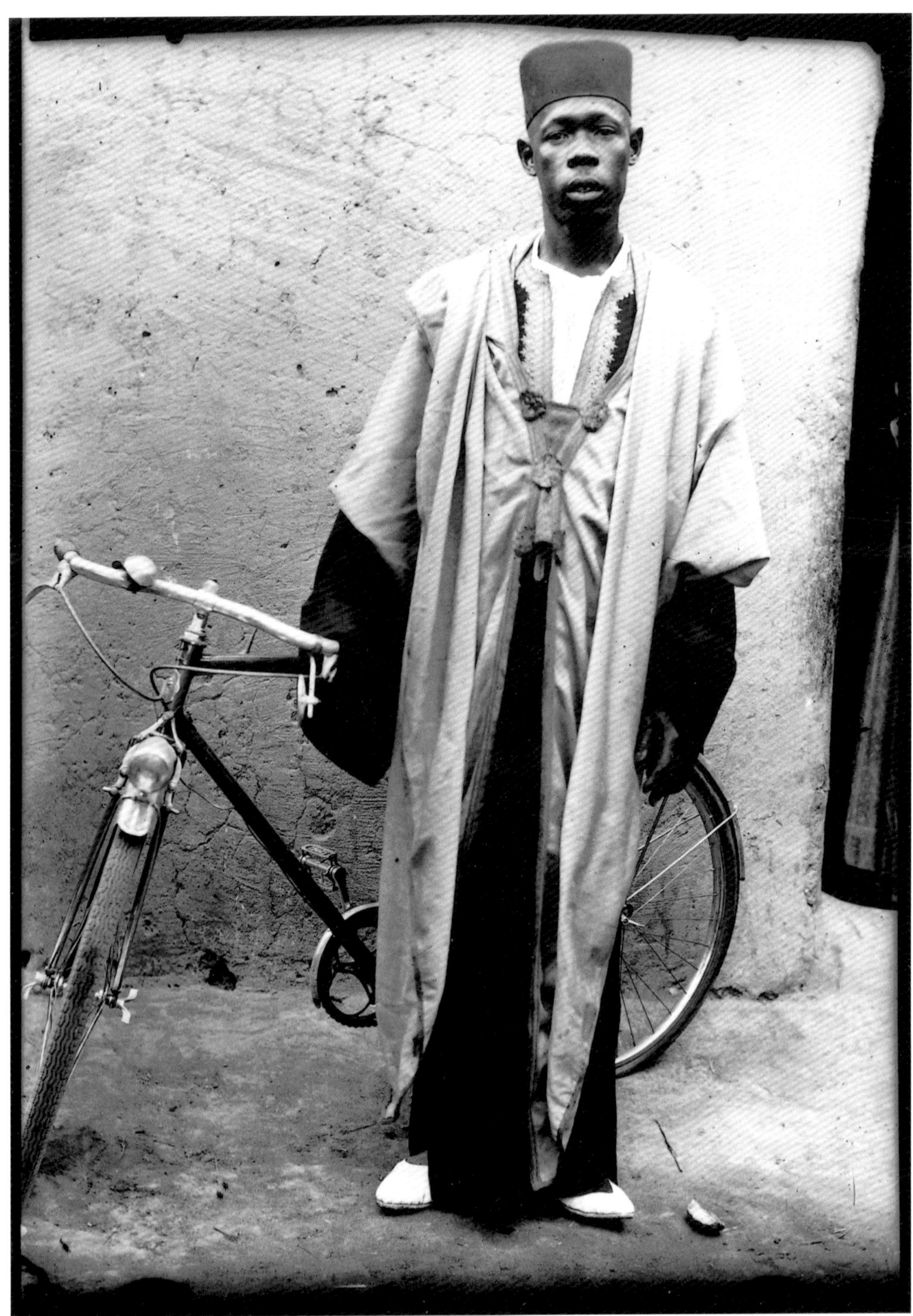

46 Seydou Keïta, *Untitled*, 1959

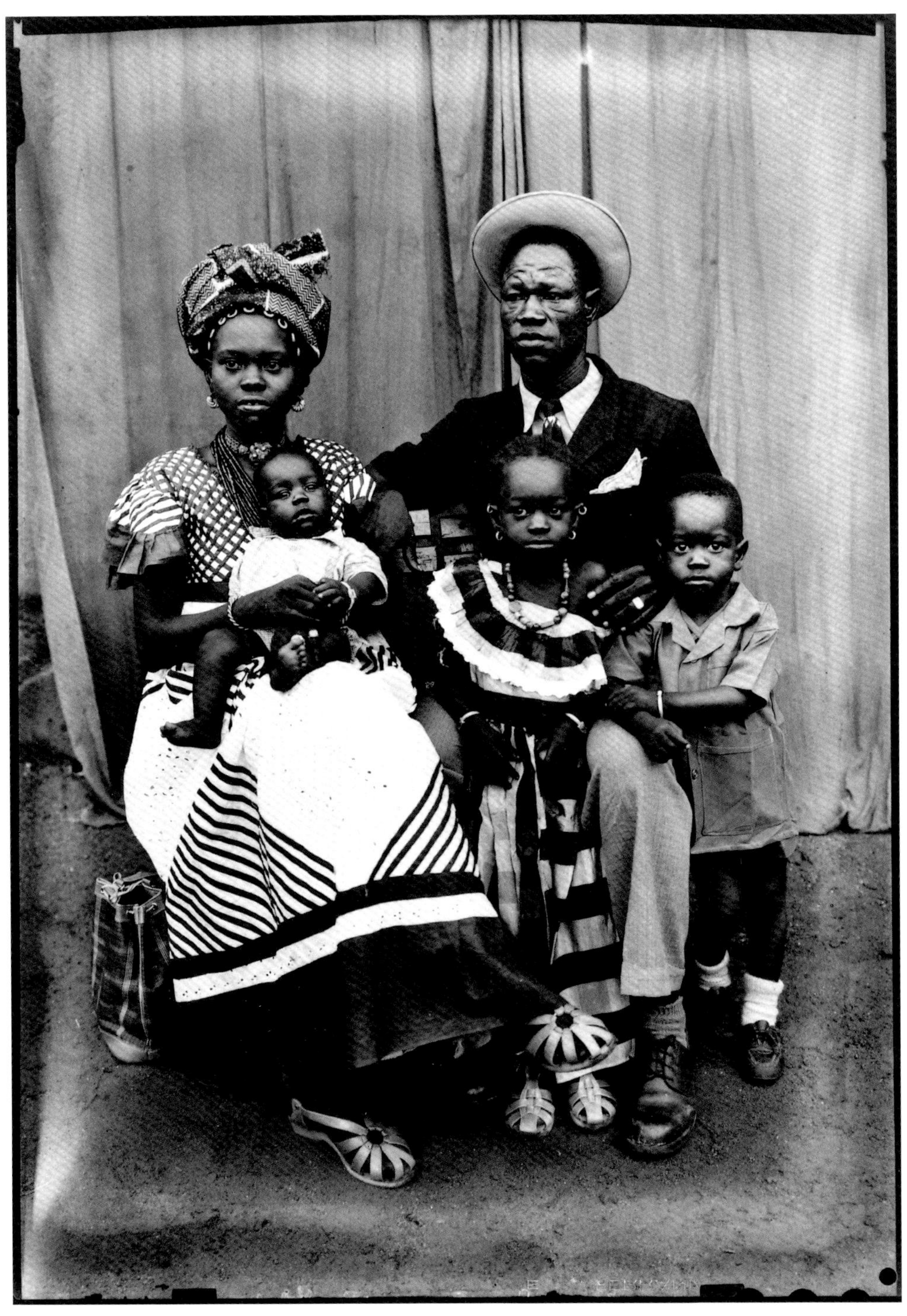

47 Seydou Keïta, *Untitled*, 1952–55

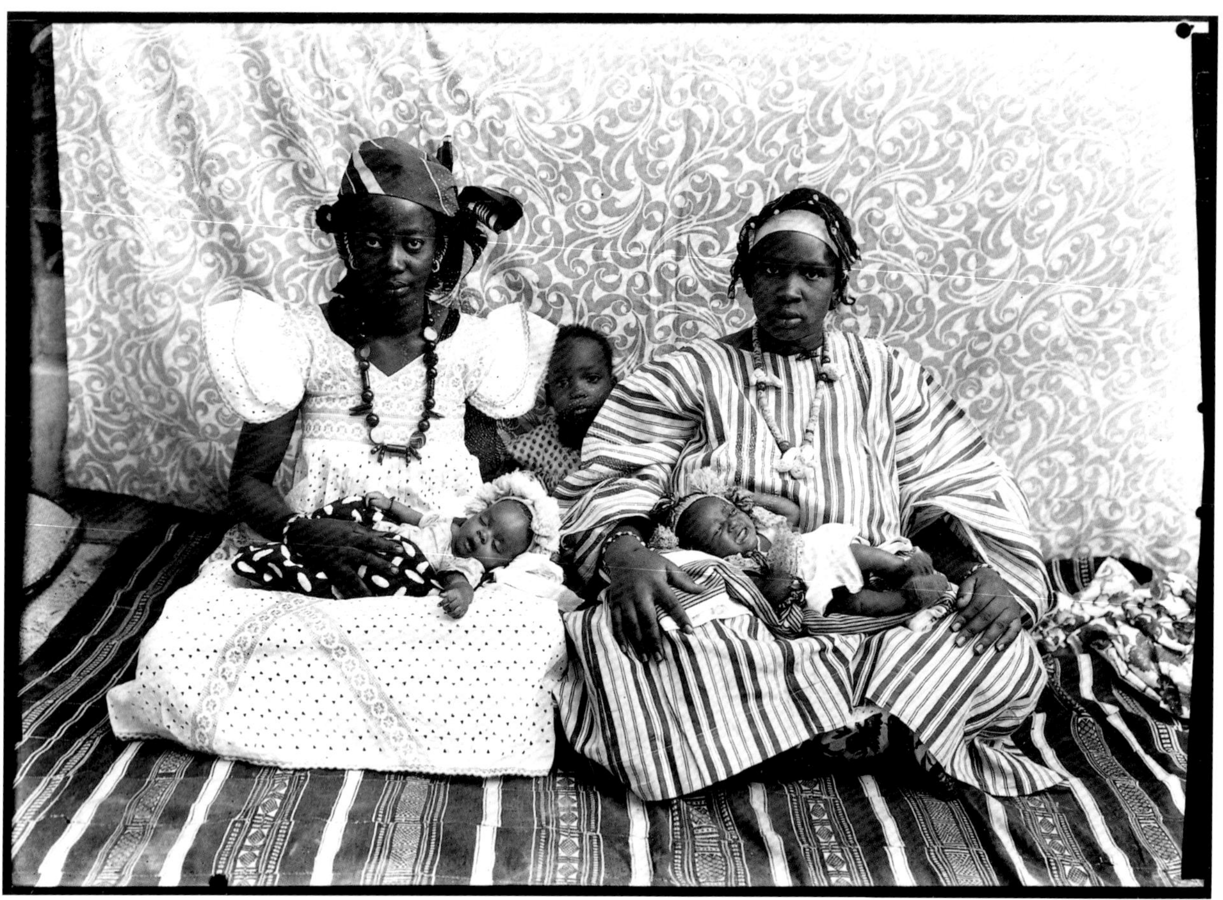

48 Seydou Keïta, *Untitled*, 1956

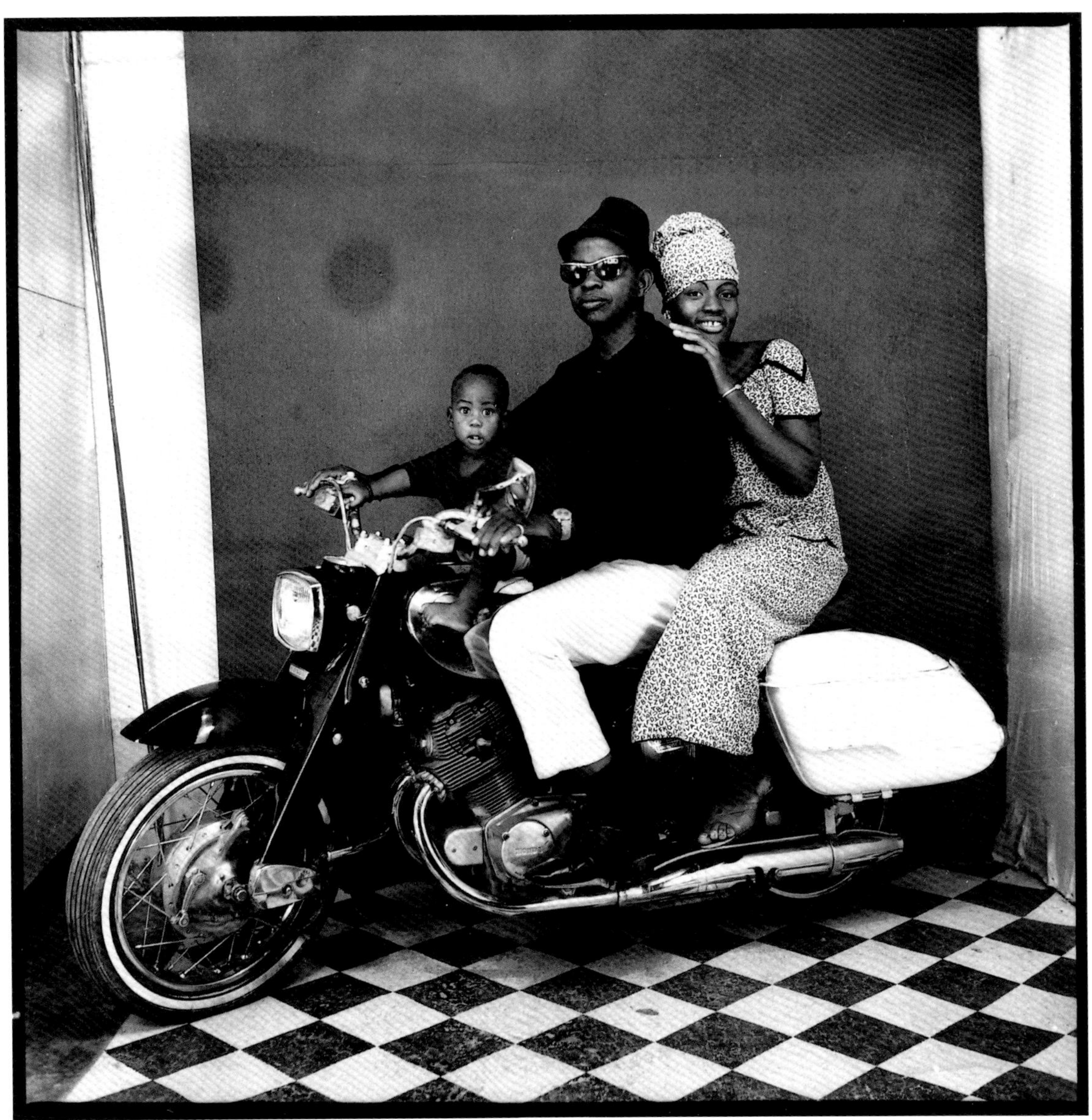

49 Malick Sidibé, *Toute la famille en moto* [The whole family on a motorcycle], 1962

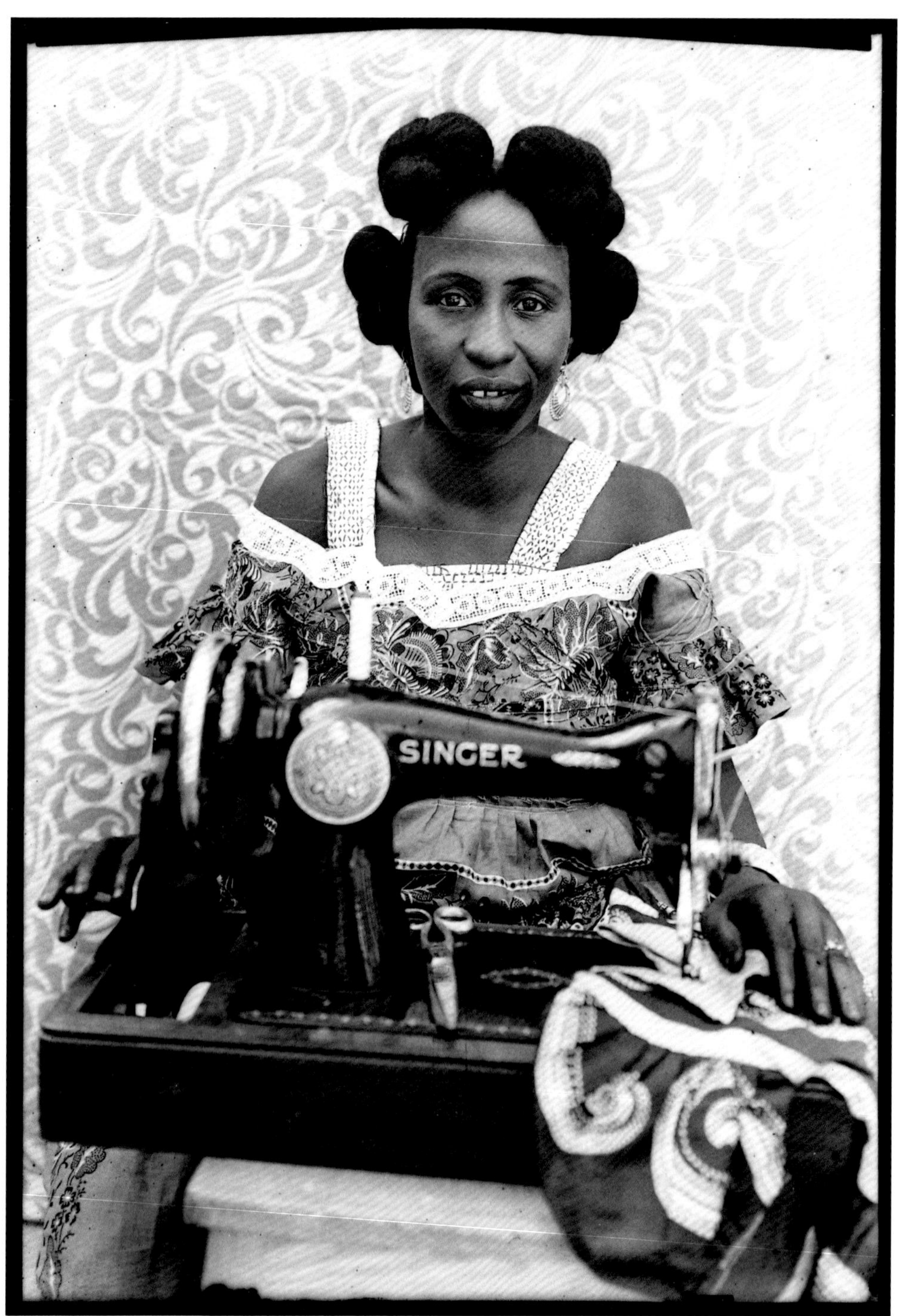

50 Seydou Keïta, *Untitled*, 1956–57

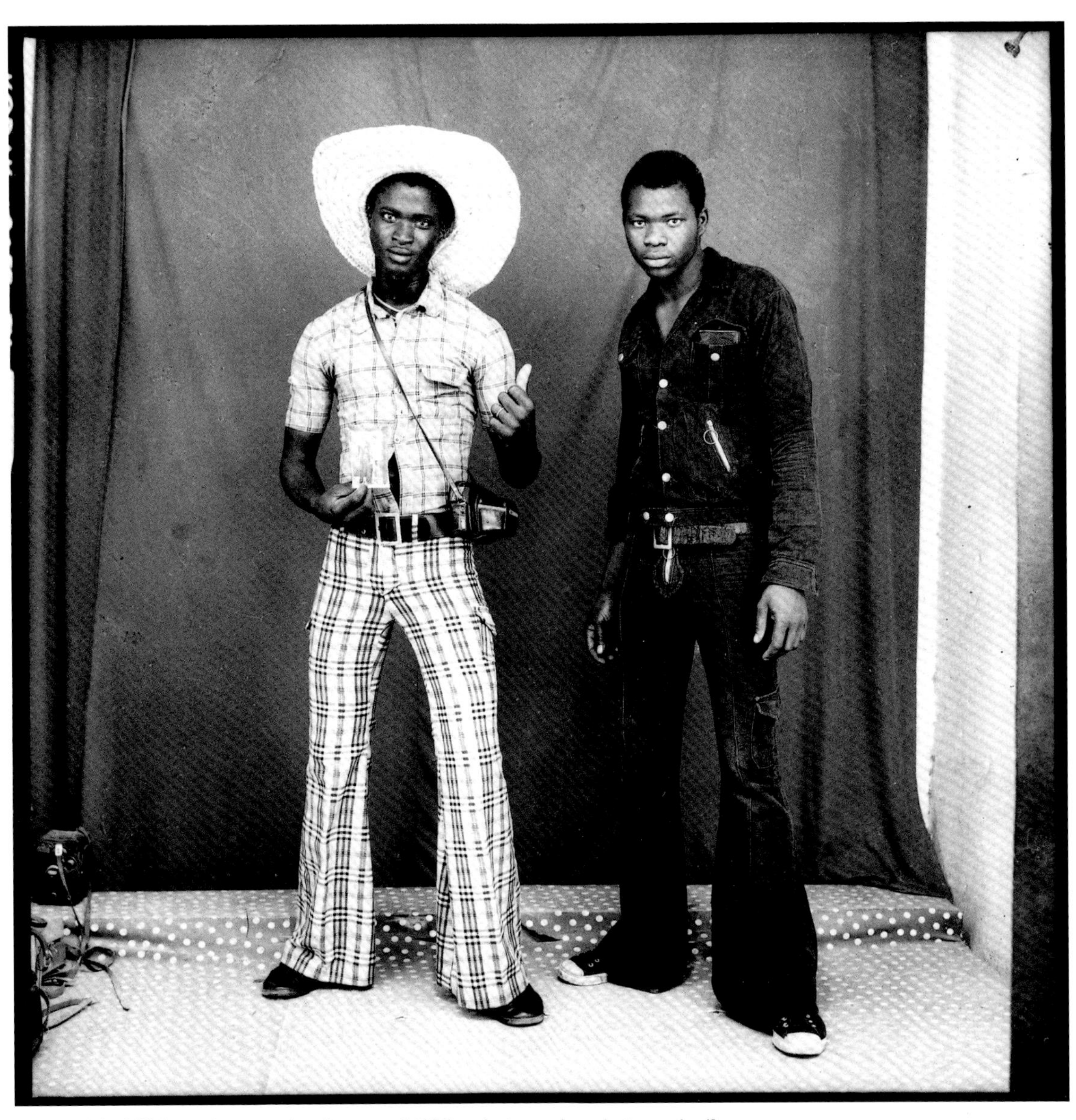

51 Malick Sidibé, *Le photographe photographié* [The photographer photographed], 1971

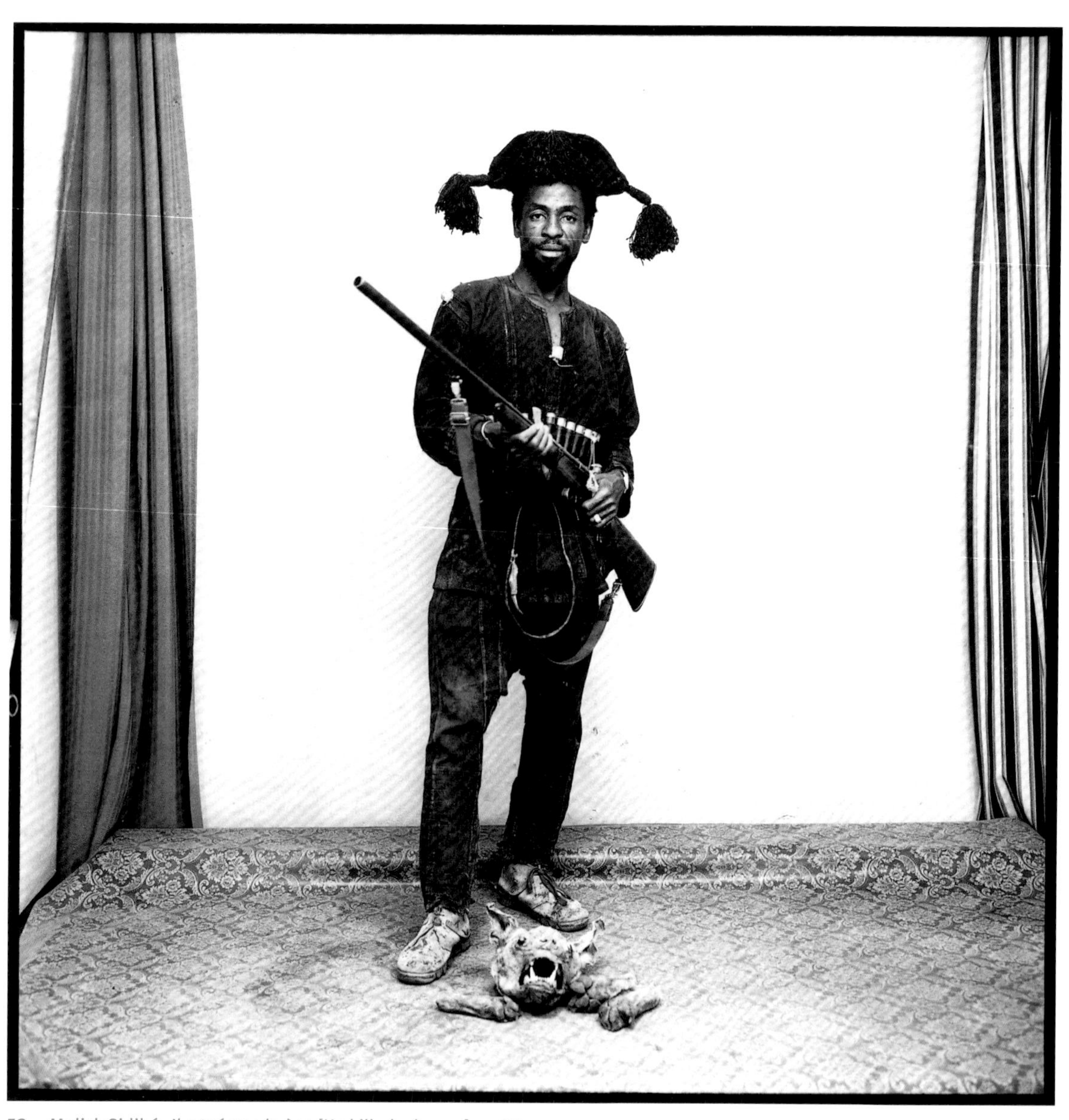

52 Malick Sidibé, *Il a tué une hyène* [He killed a hyena], 1986

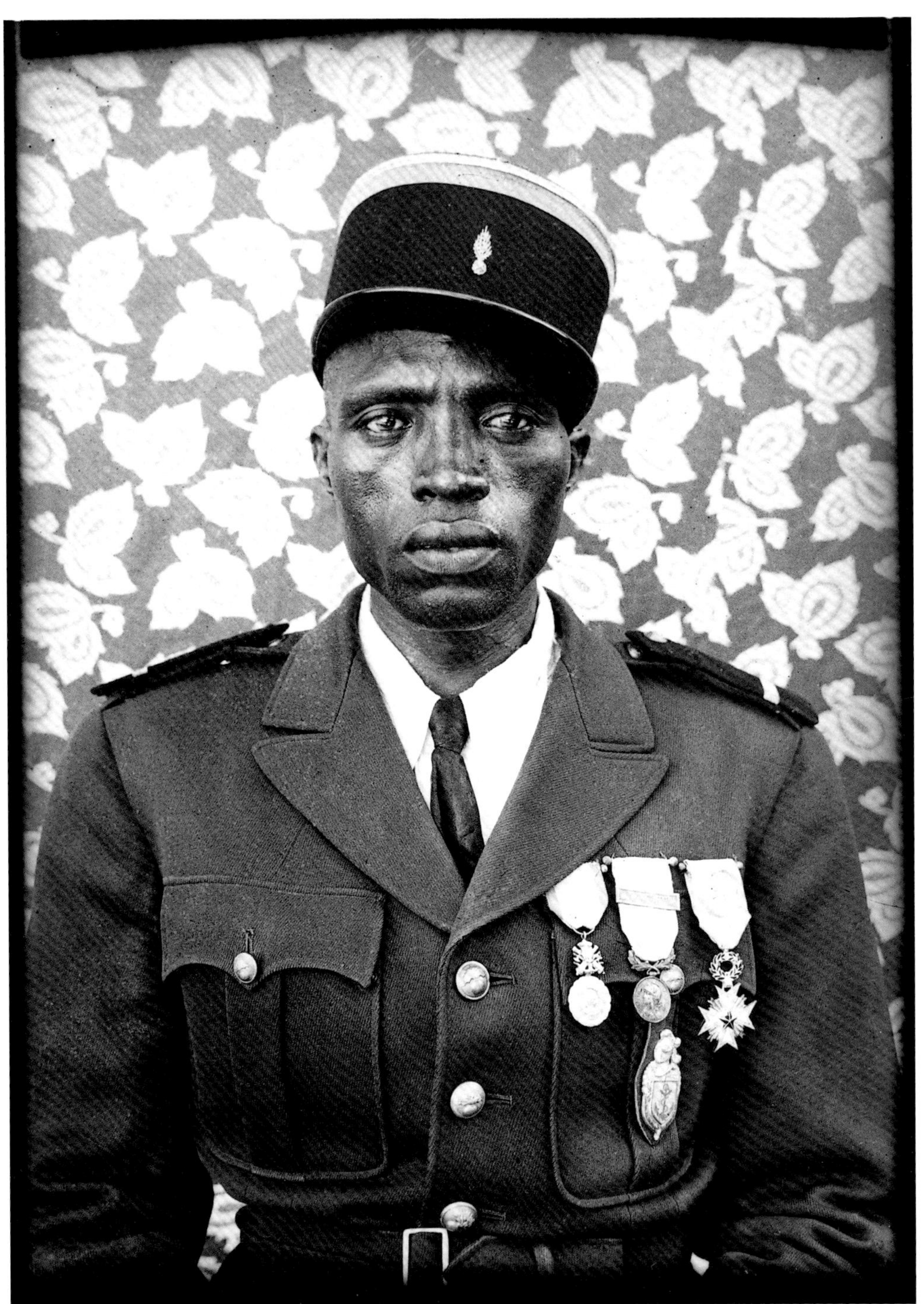

53 Seydou Keïta, *Untitled*, 1957

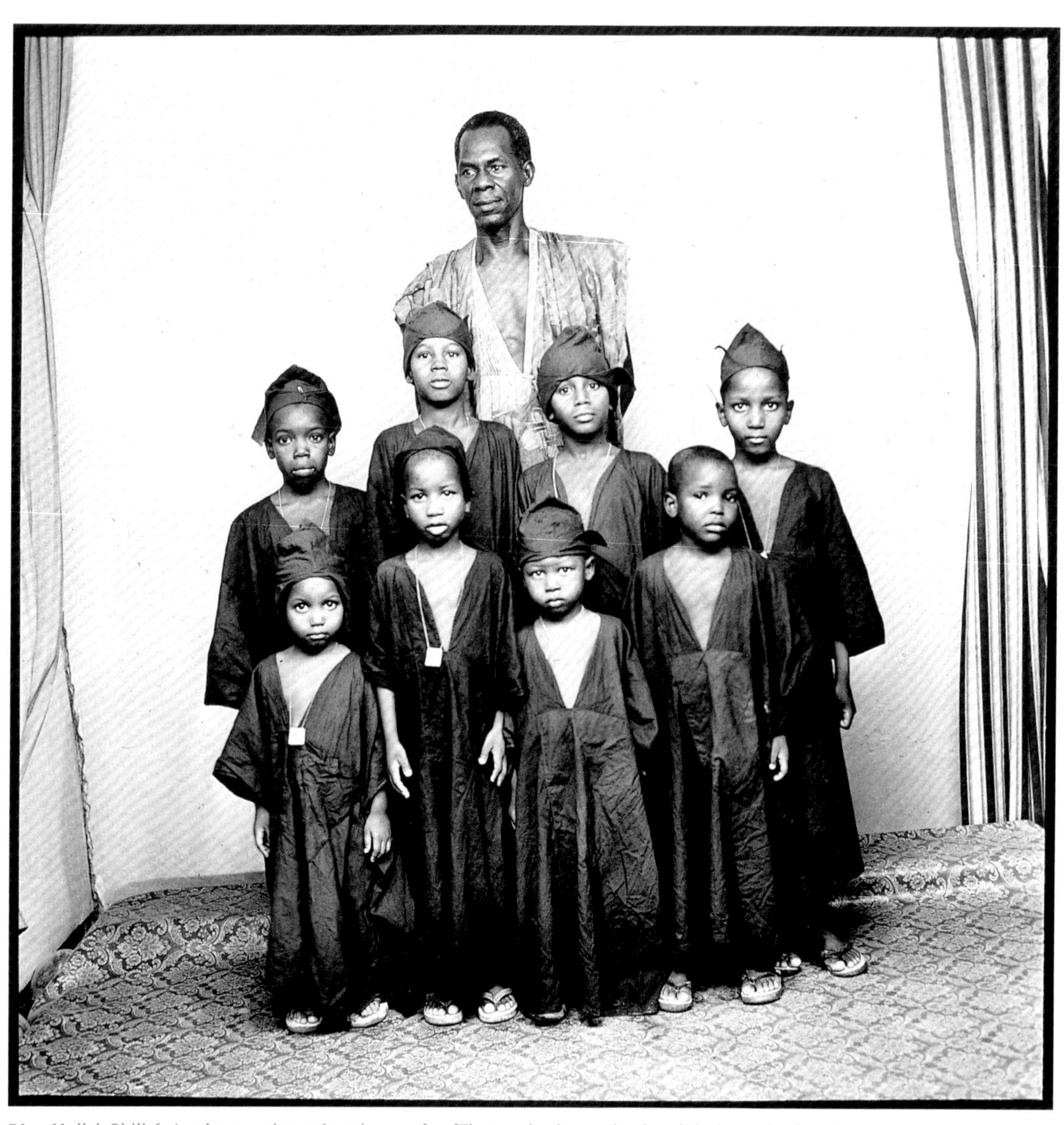

54 Malick Sidibé, *Les jeunes circoncis et leur maître* [The newly circumcised and their teacher], 1983

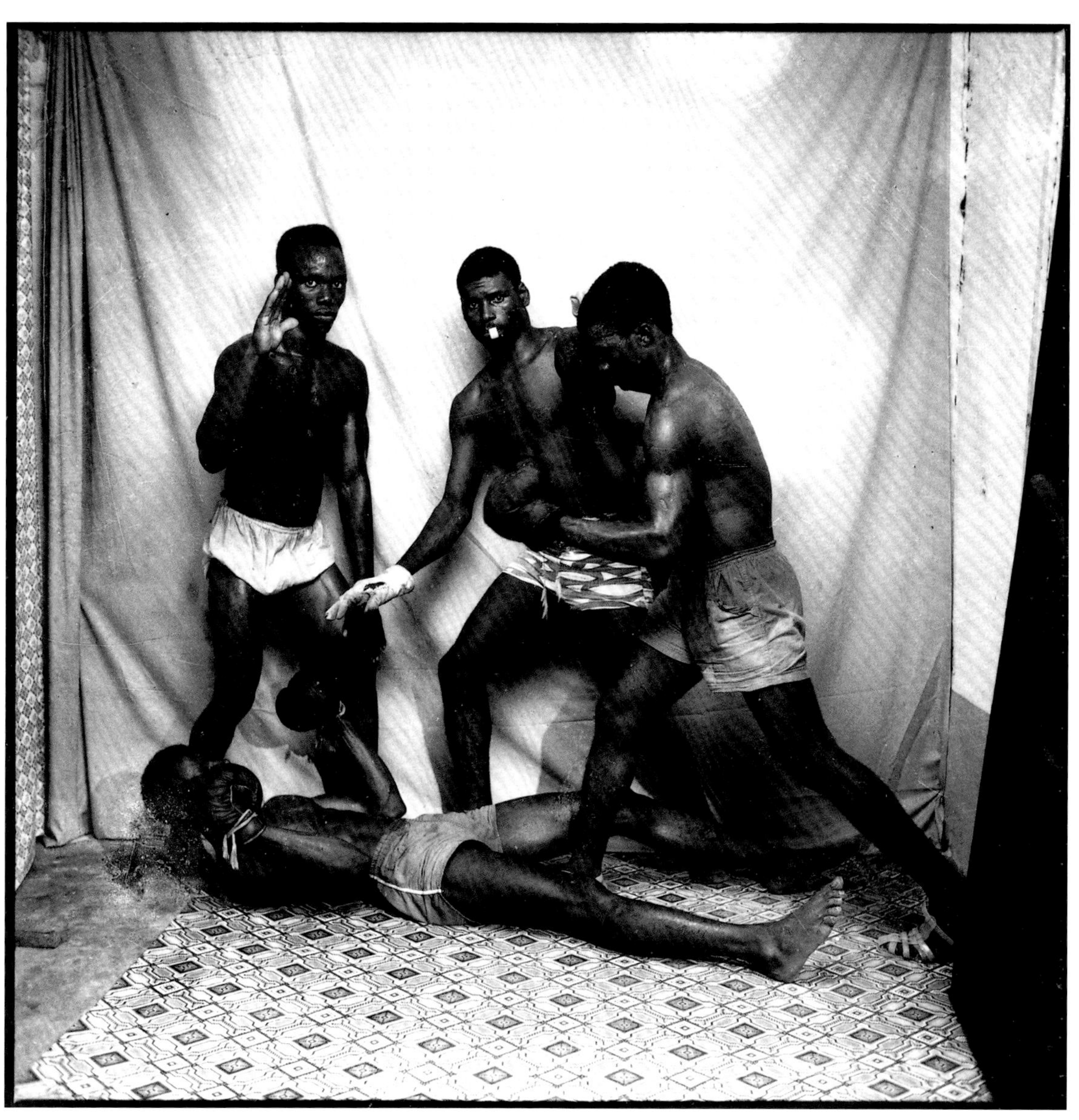

55 Malick Sidibé, *Boxeurs en démonstration* [Boxers giving a demonstration], 1965

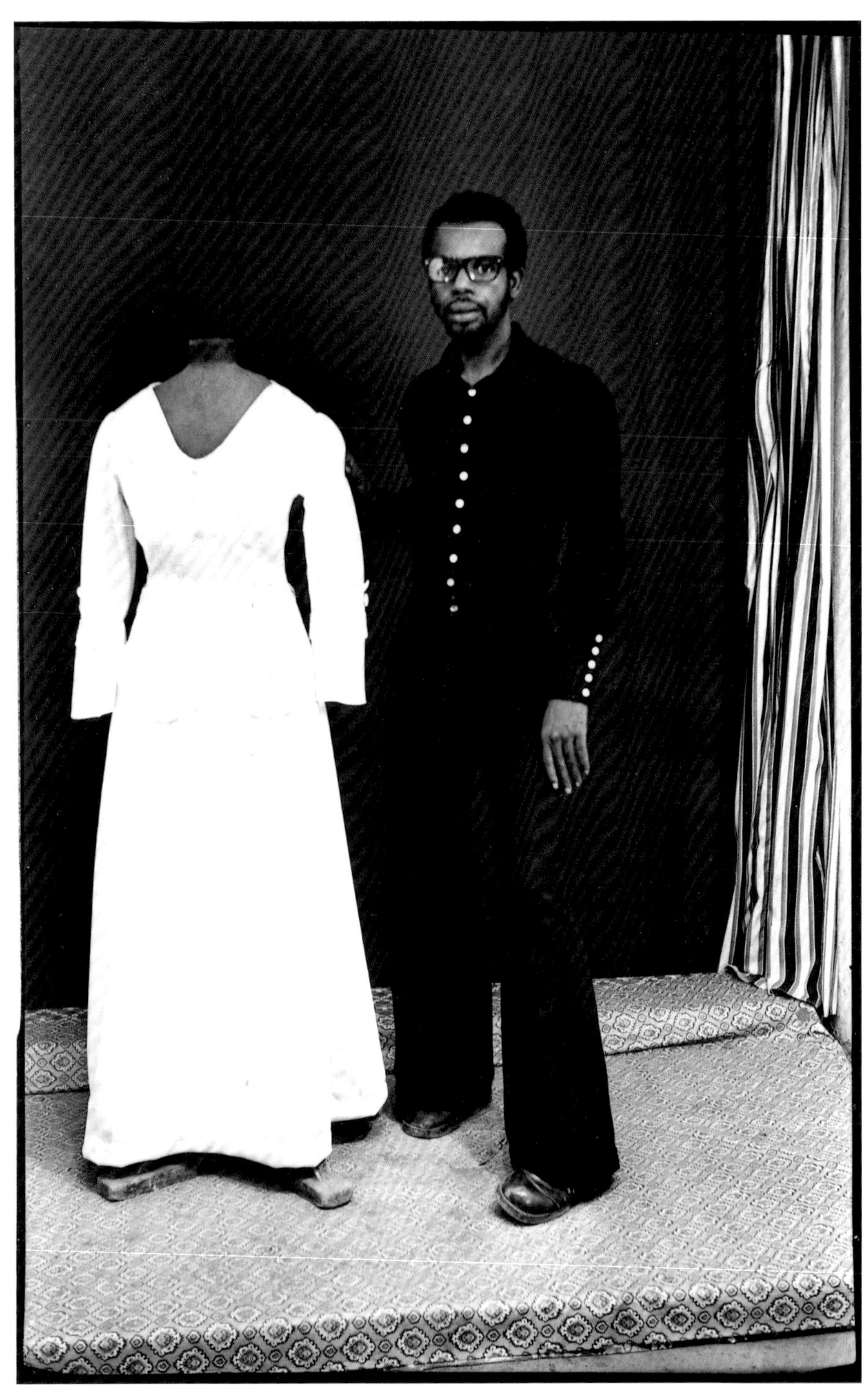

56 Malick Sidibé, *Tailleur et son modèle* [Tailor and his model], 1974

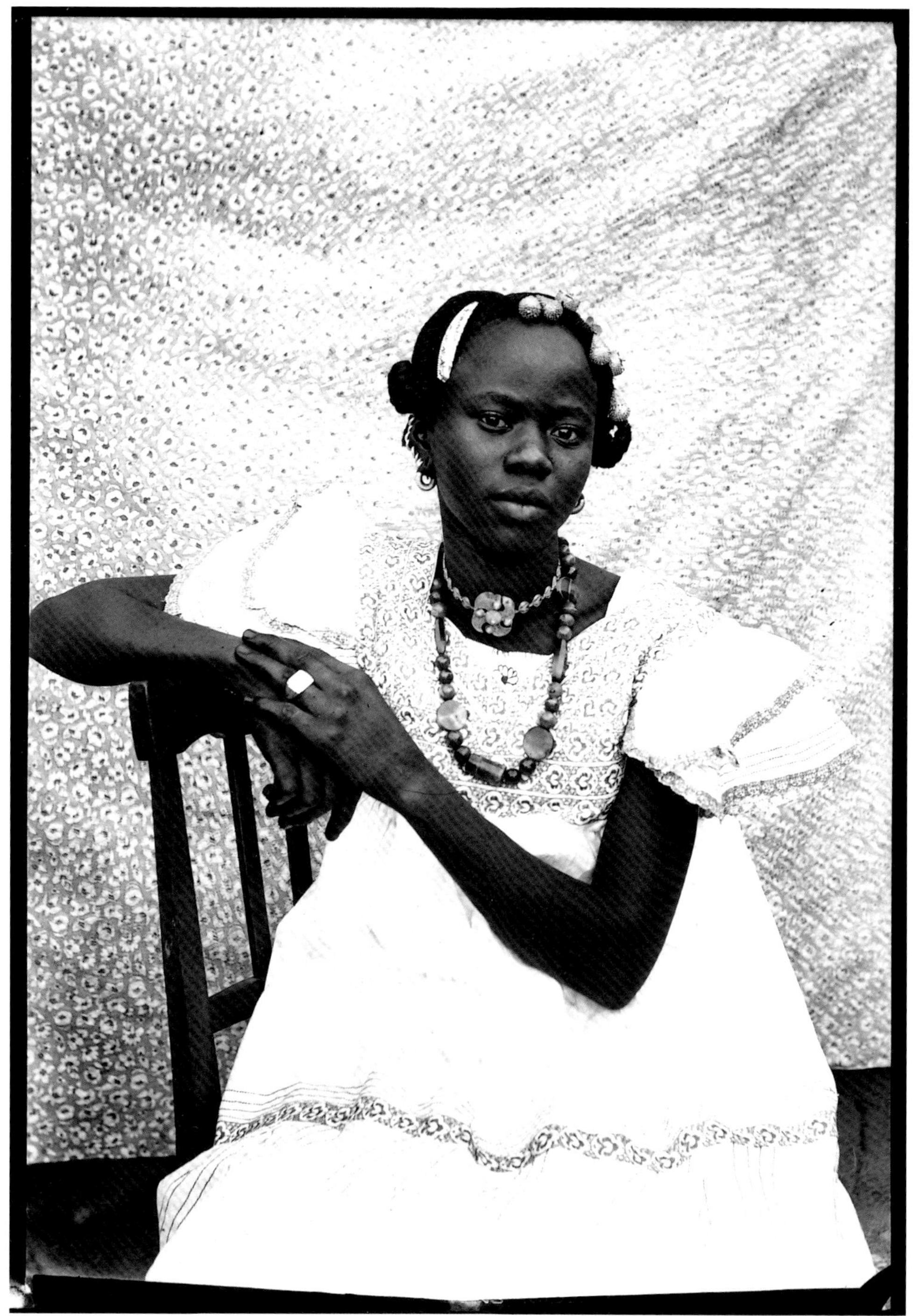

57 Seydou Keïta, *Untitled*, 1959

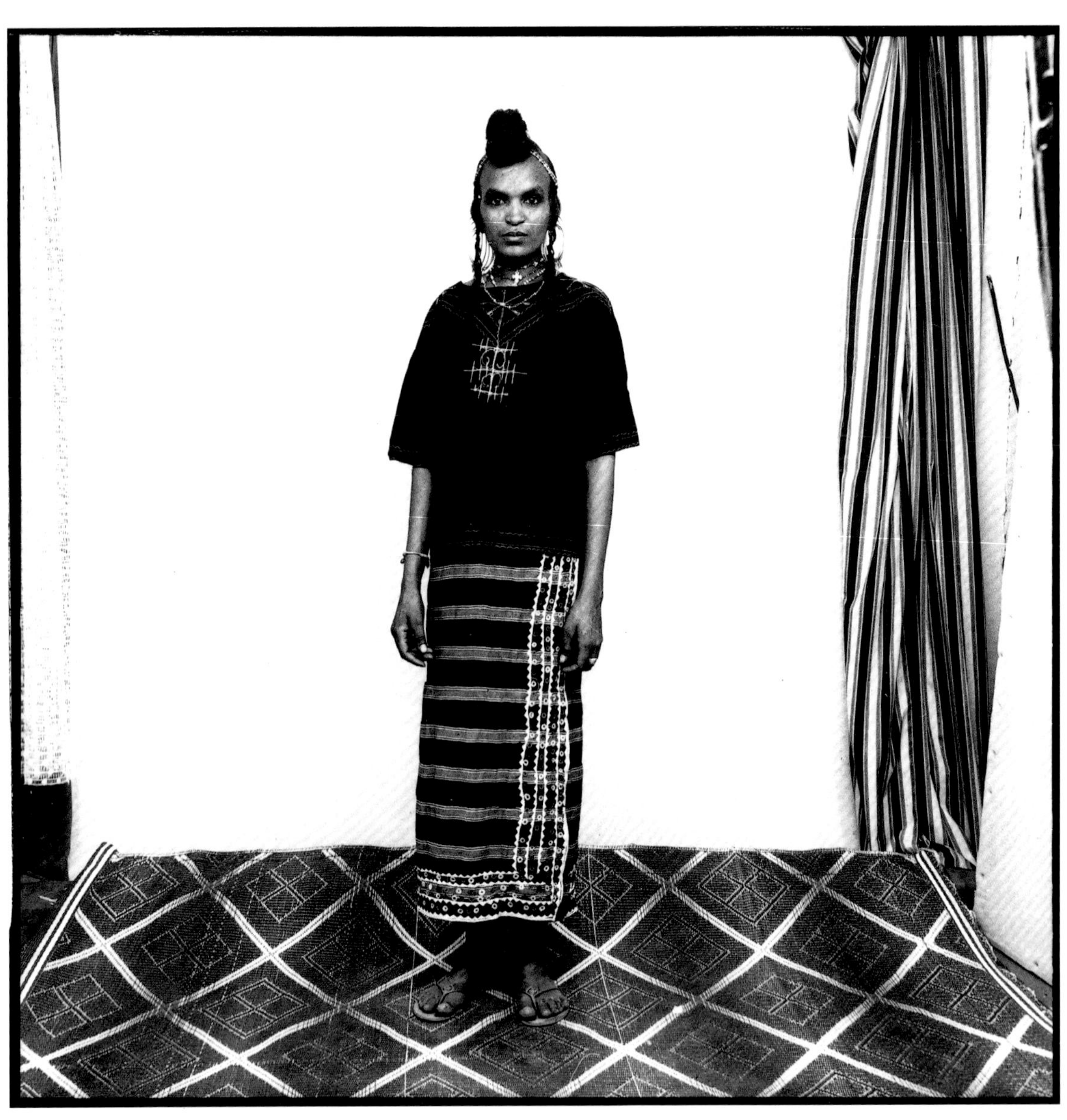

58 Malick Sidibé, *Femme Peuhl du Niger* [Peul woman from Niger], 1970

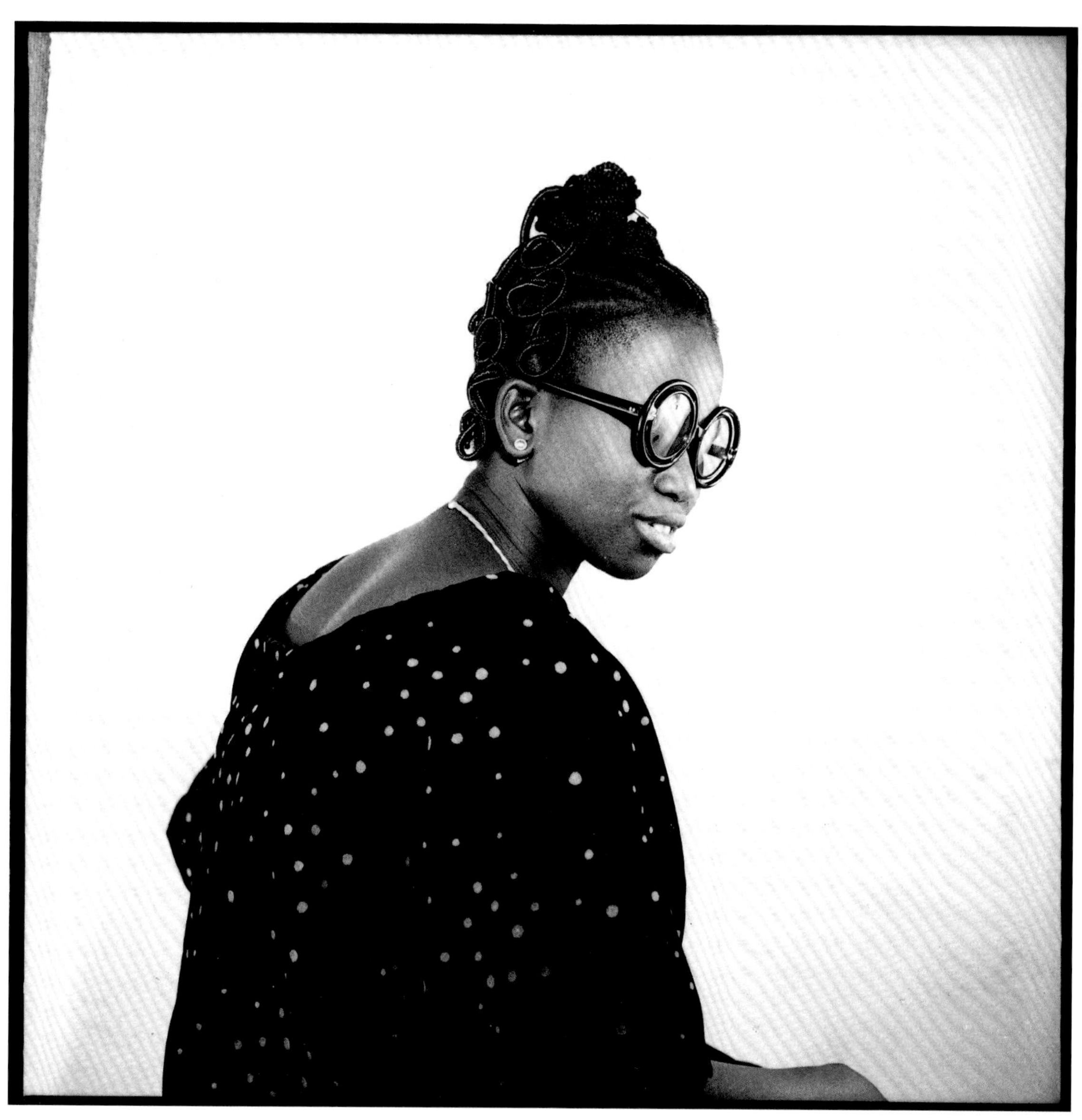

59 Malick Sidibé, *Portrait de Mlle Kanté Sira* [Portrait of Miss Kanté Sira], 1965

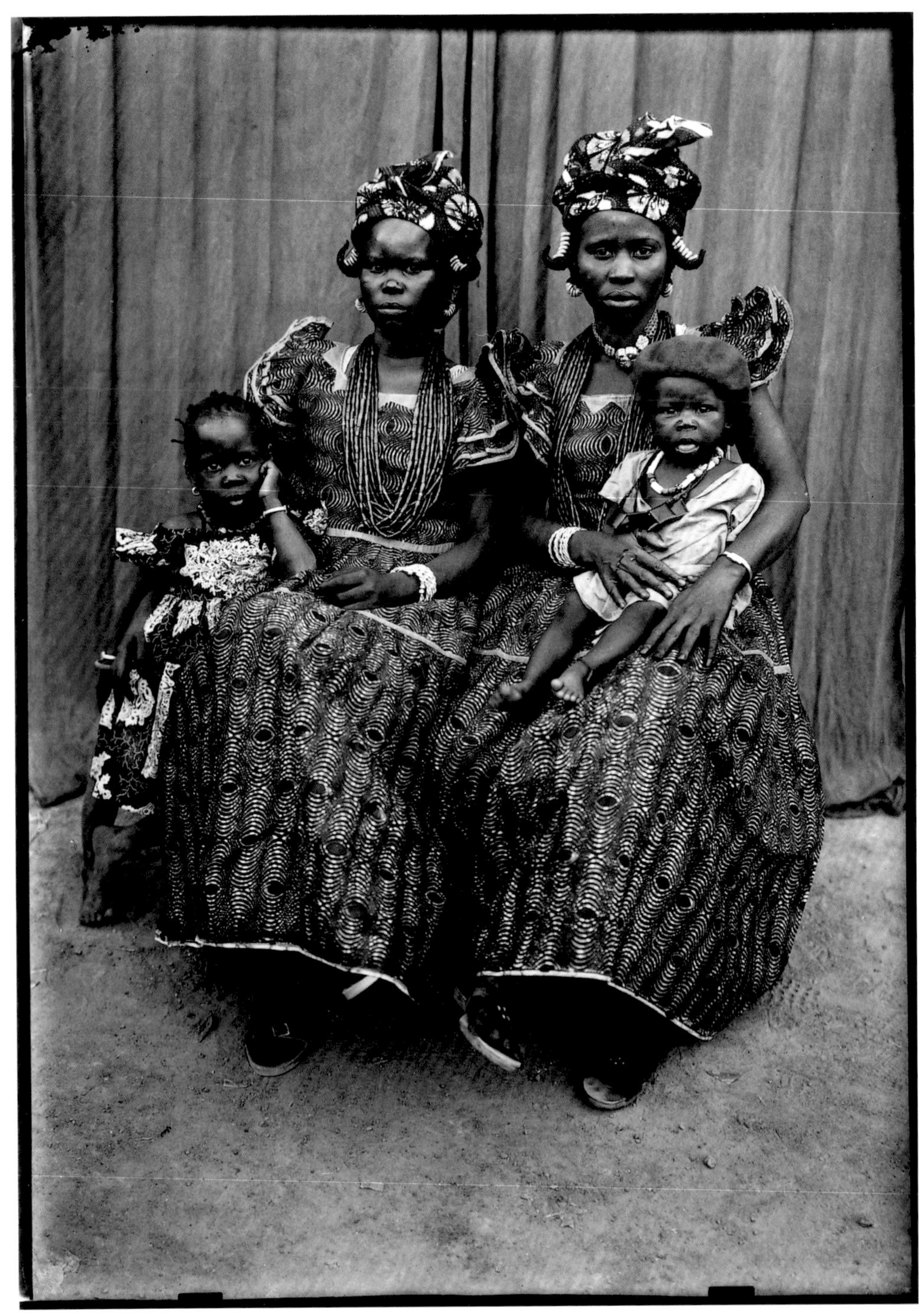

60 Seydou Keïta, *Untitled*, 1952–55

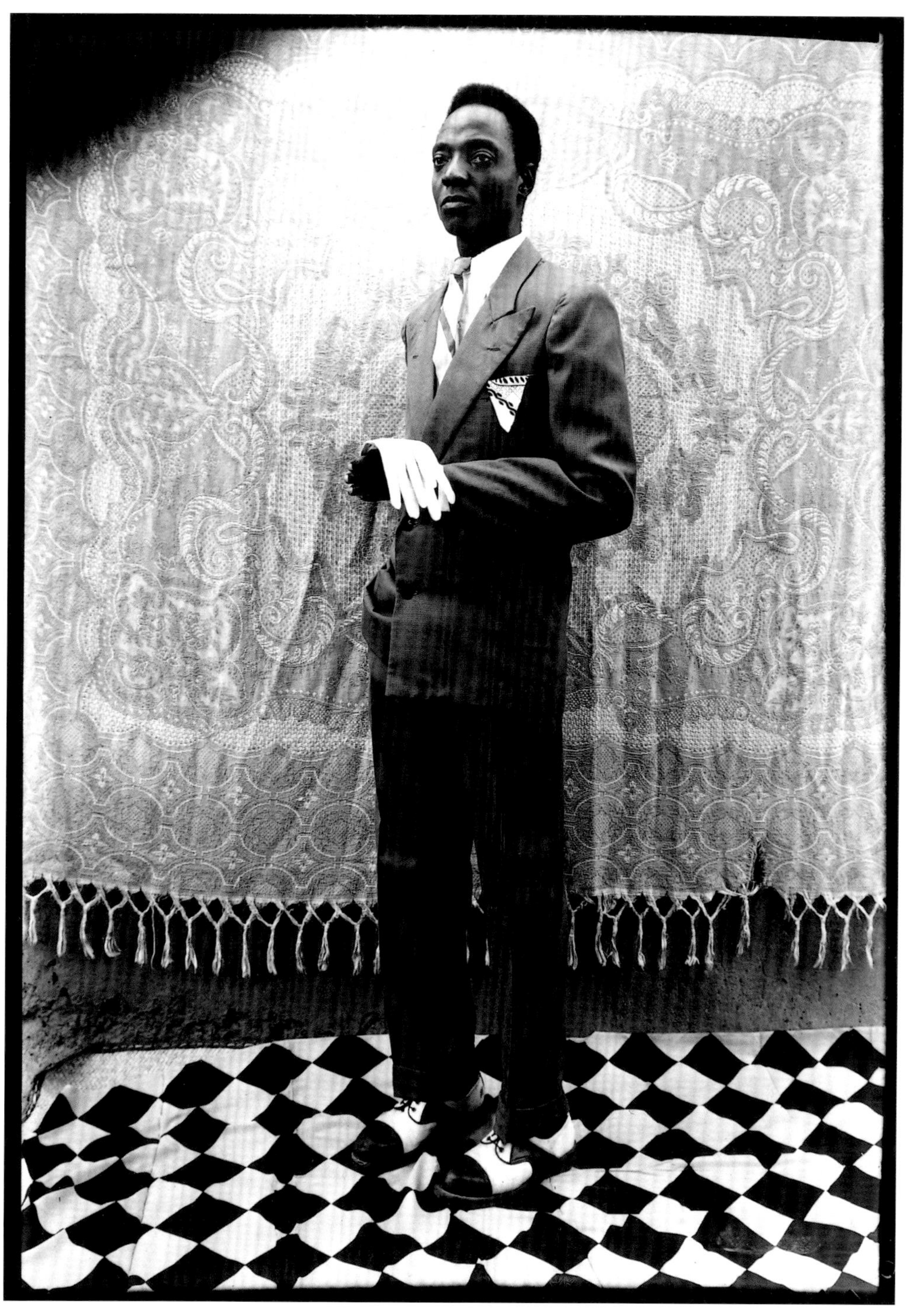

61 Seydou Keïta, *Untitled*, 1949–51

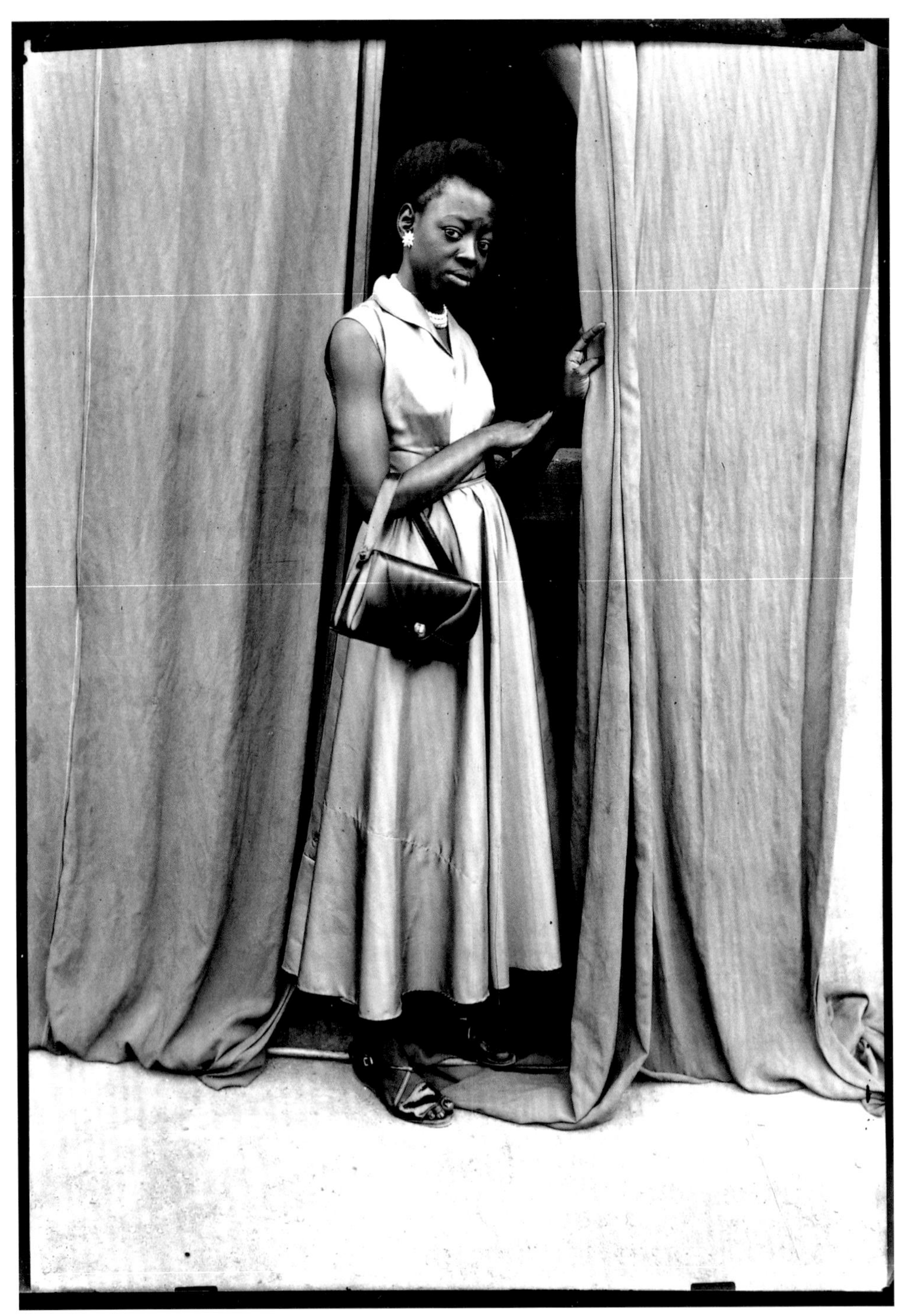

62 Seydou Keïta, *Untitled*, 1952–55

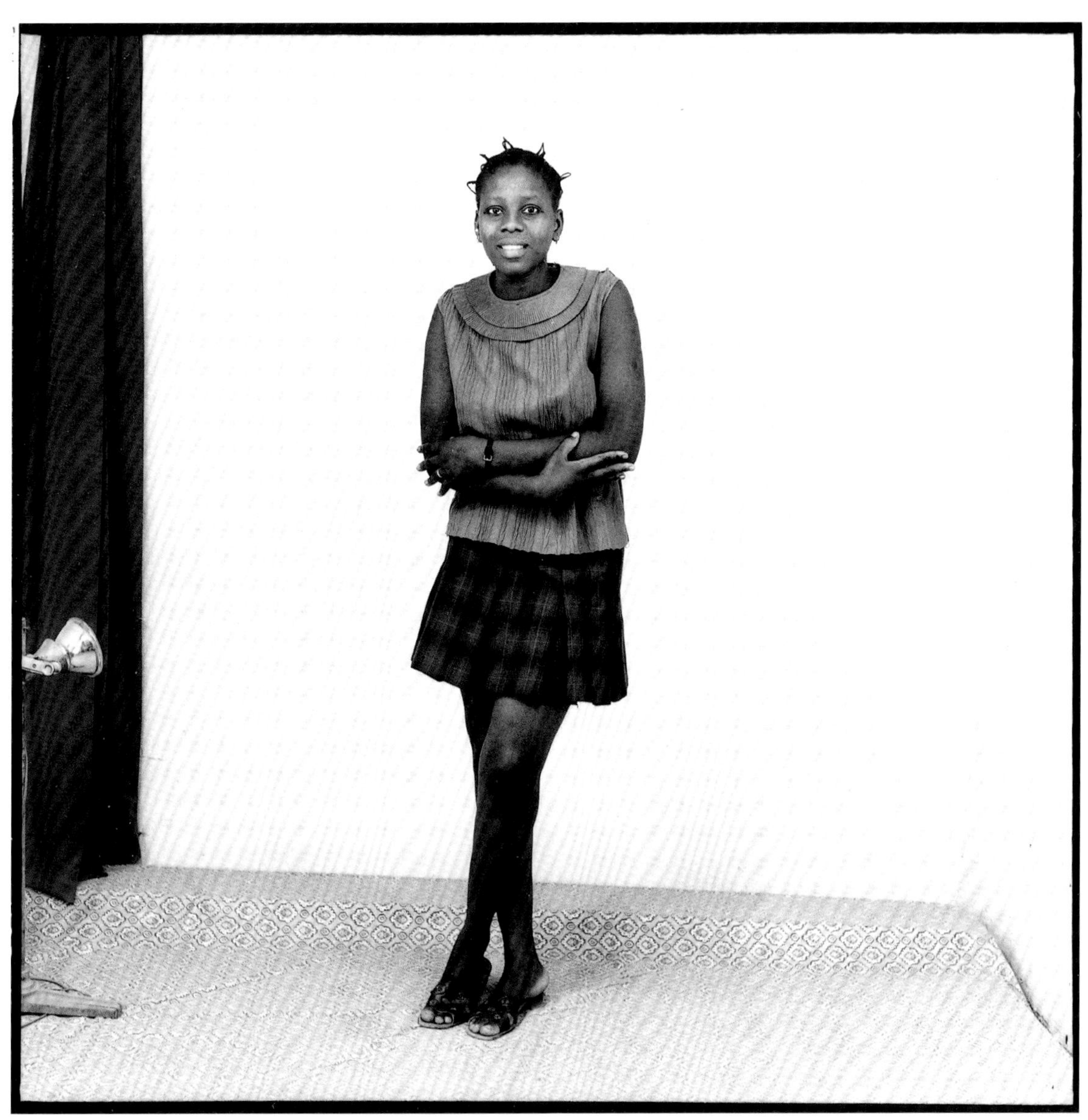

63 Malick Sidibé, *Je suis bien comme ça!* [I look good like this!], n.d.

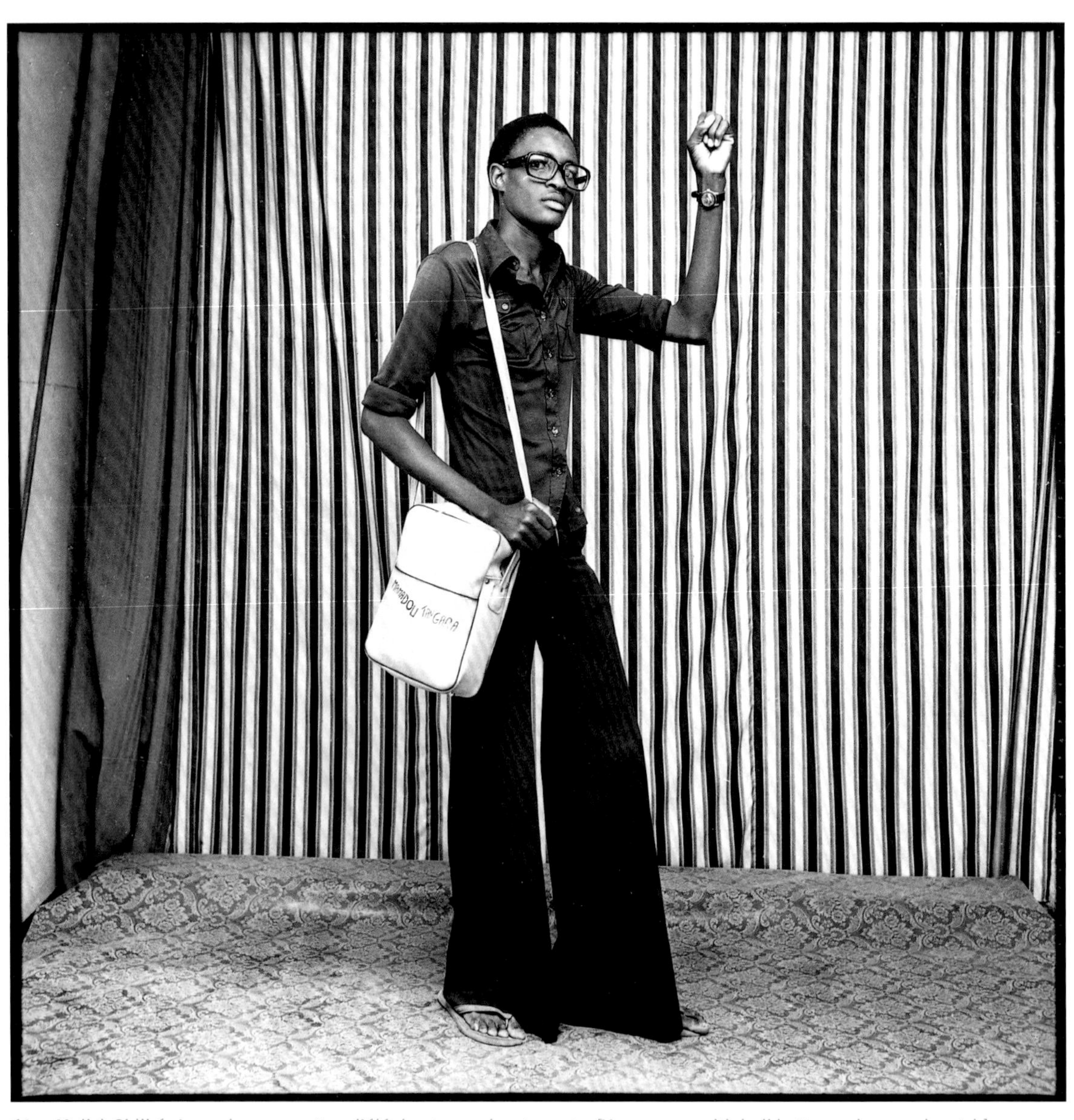

64 Malick Sidibé, *Jeune homme pattes d'éléphant sacoche et montre* [Young man with bell bottoms, bag, and watch], 1977

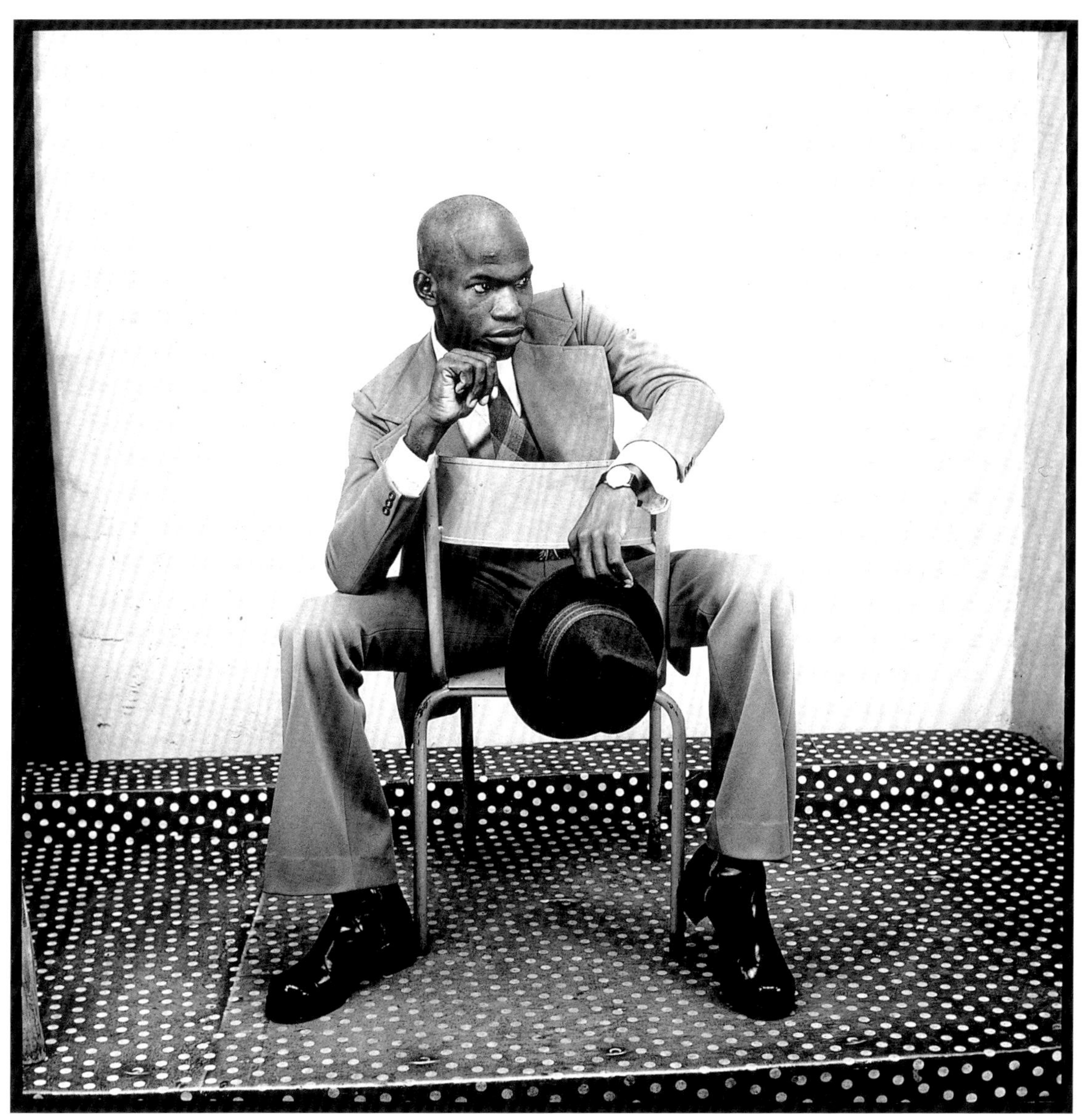

65 Malick Sidibé, *Un tailleur gentleman surnommé Mabus* [A gentleman tailor by the name of Mabus], 1972

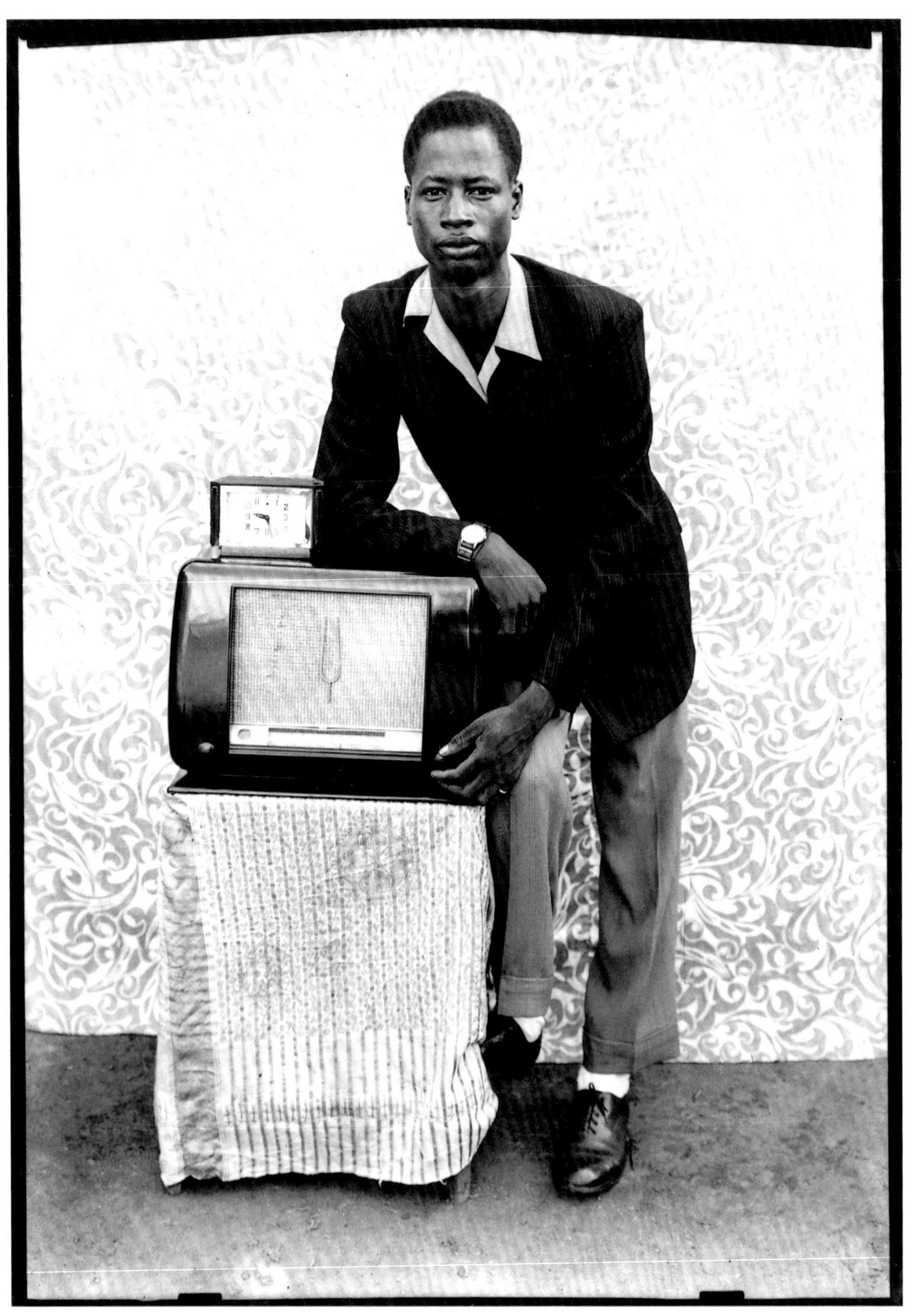

66 Seydou Keïta, *Untitled*, 1956–57

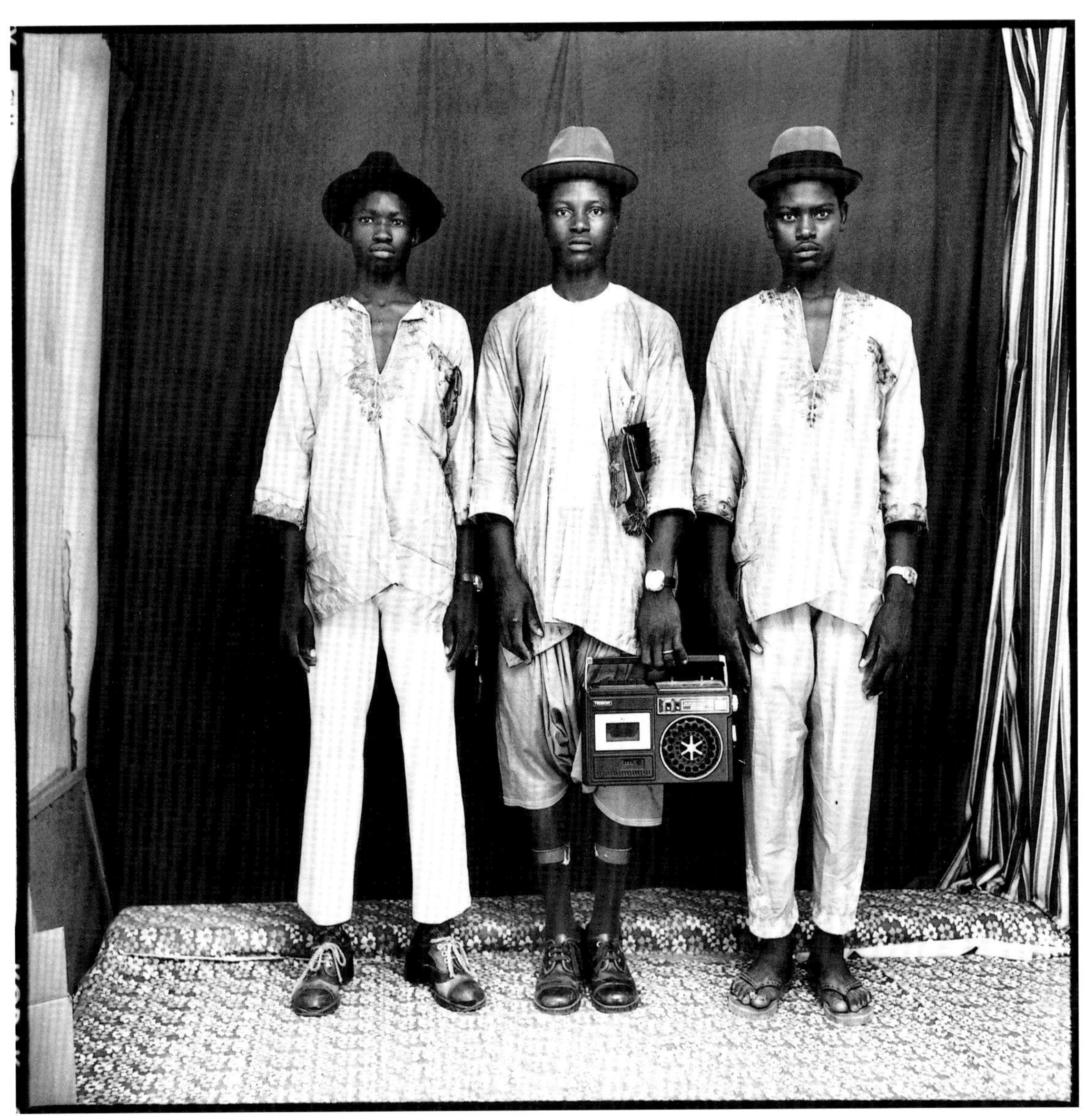

67 Malick Sidibé, *Les jeunes bergers Peuhls* [Young Peul shepherds], 1972

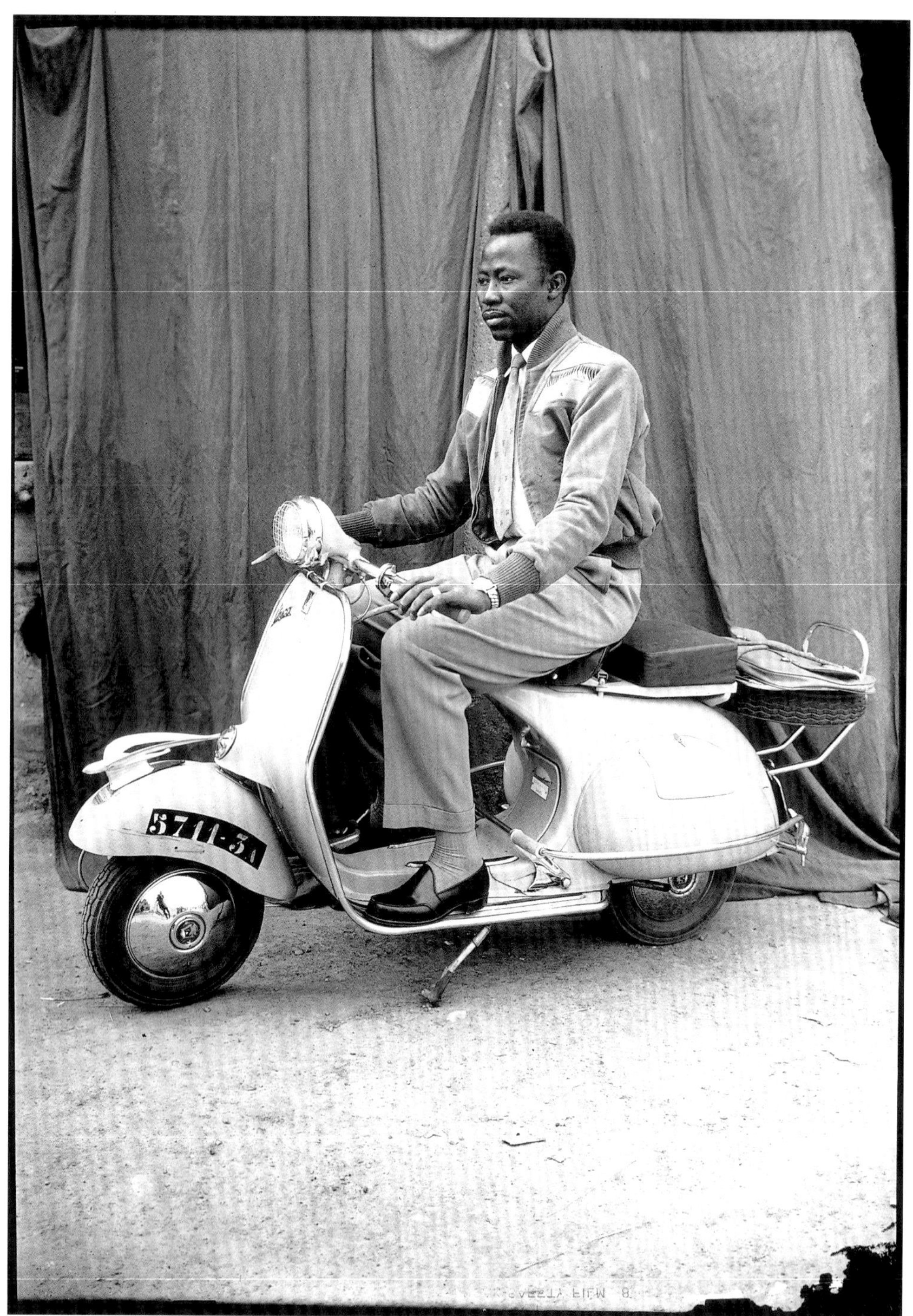

68 Seydou Keïta, *Untitled*, 1959

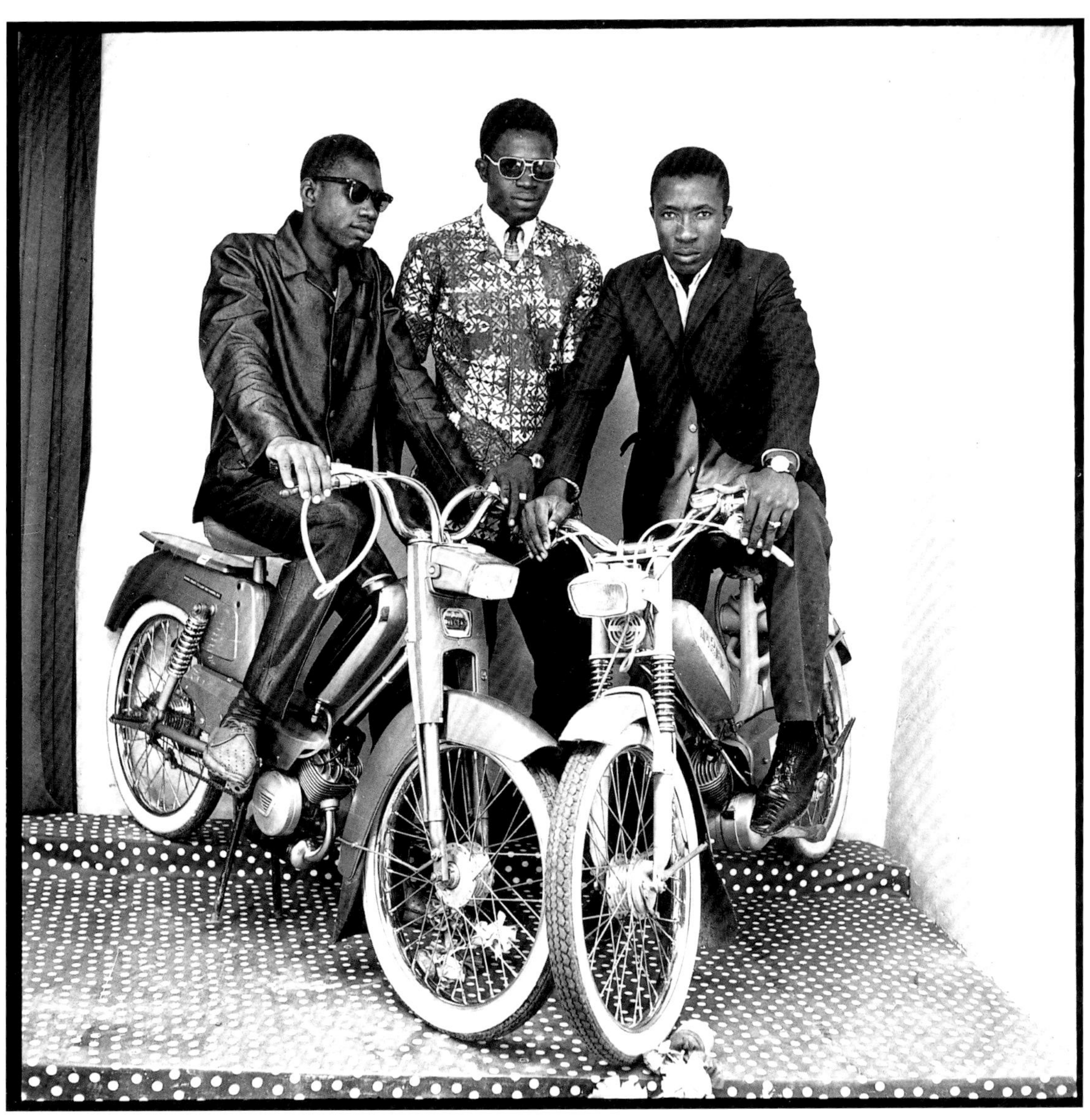

69 Malick Sidibé, *Les trois amis avec motos, studio* [Three friends with motorbikes, studio], 1975

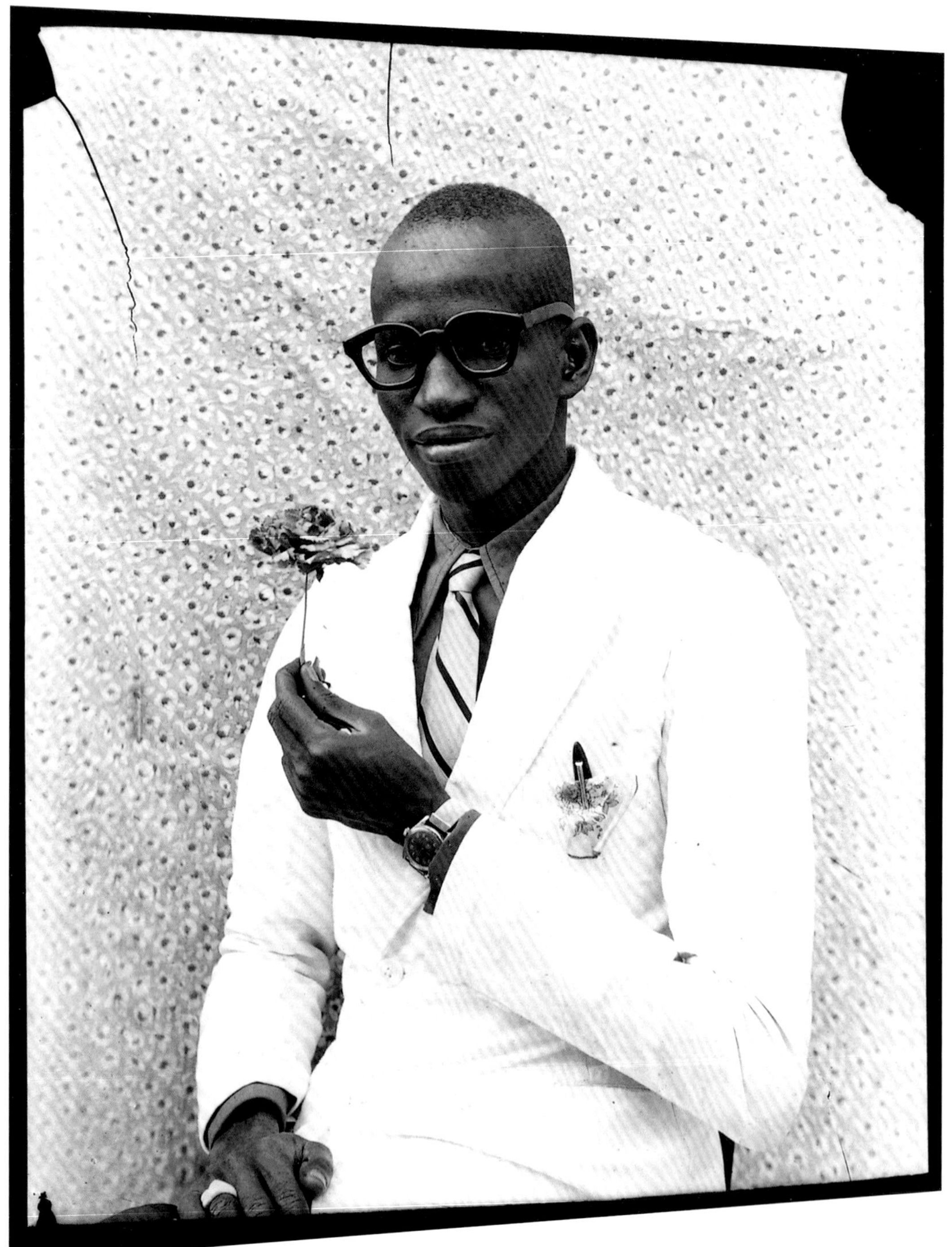

70 Seydou Keïta, *Untitled*, 1958

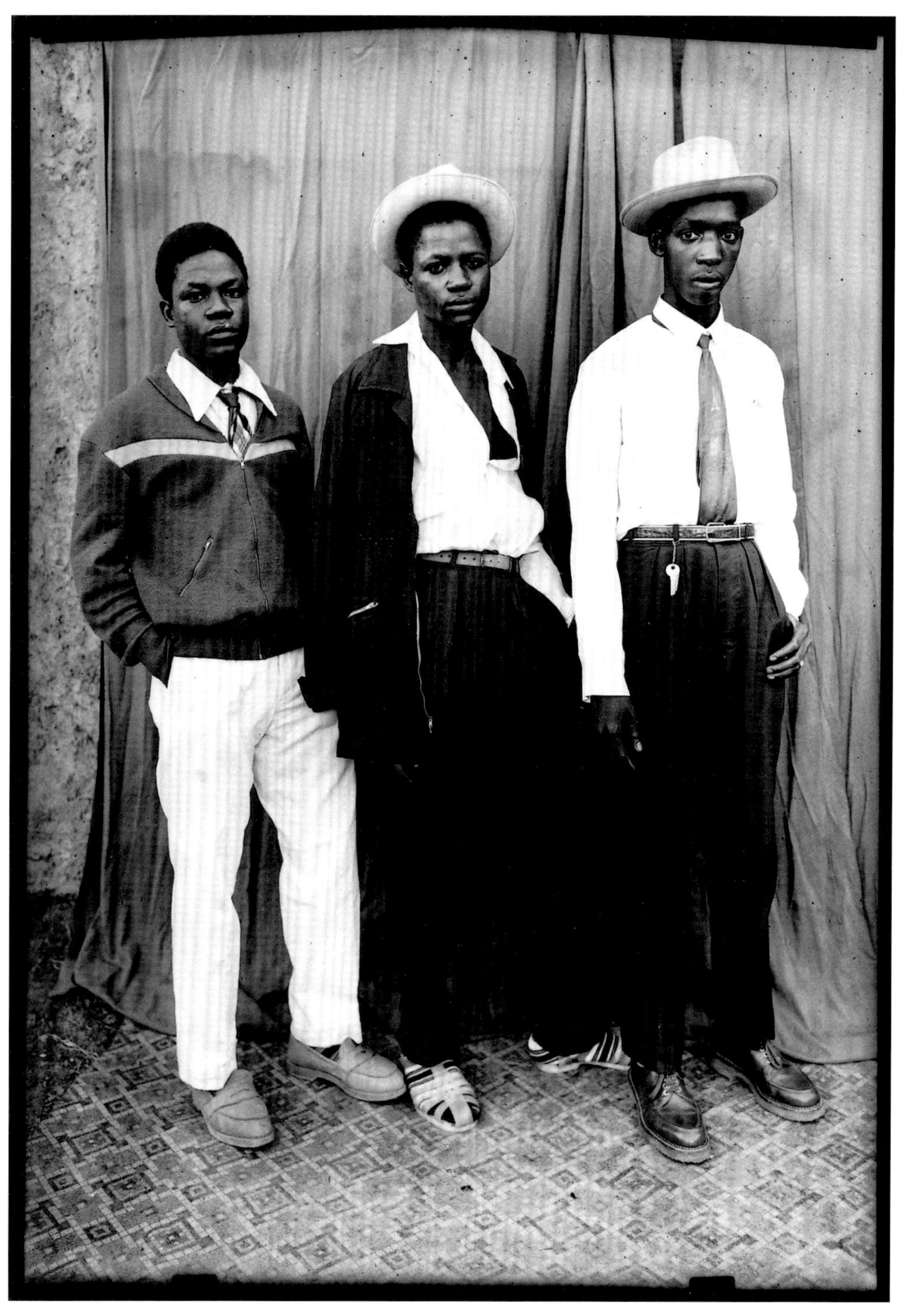

71 Seydou Keïta, *Untitled*, 1952–55

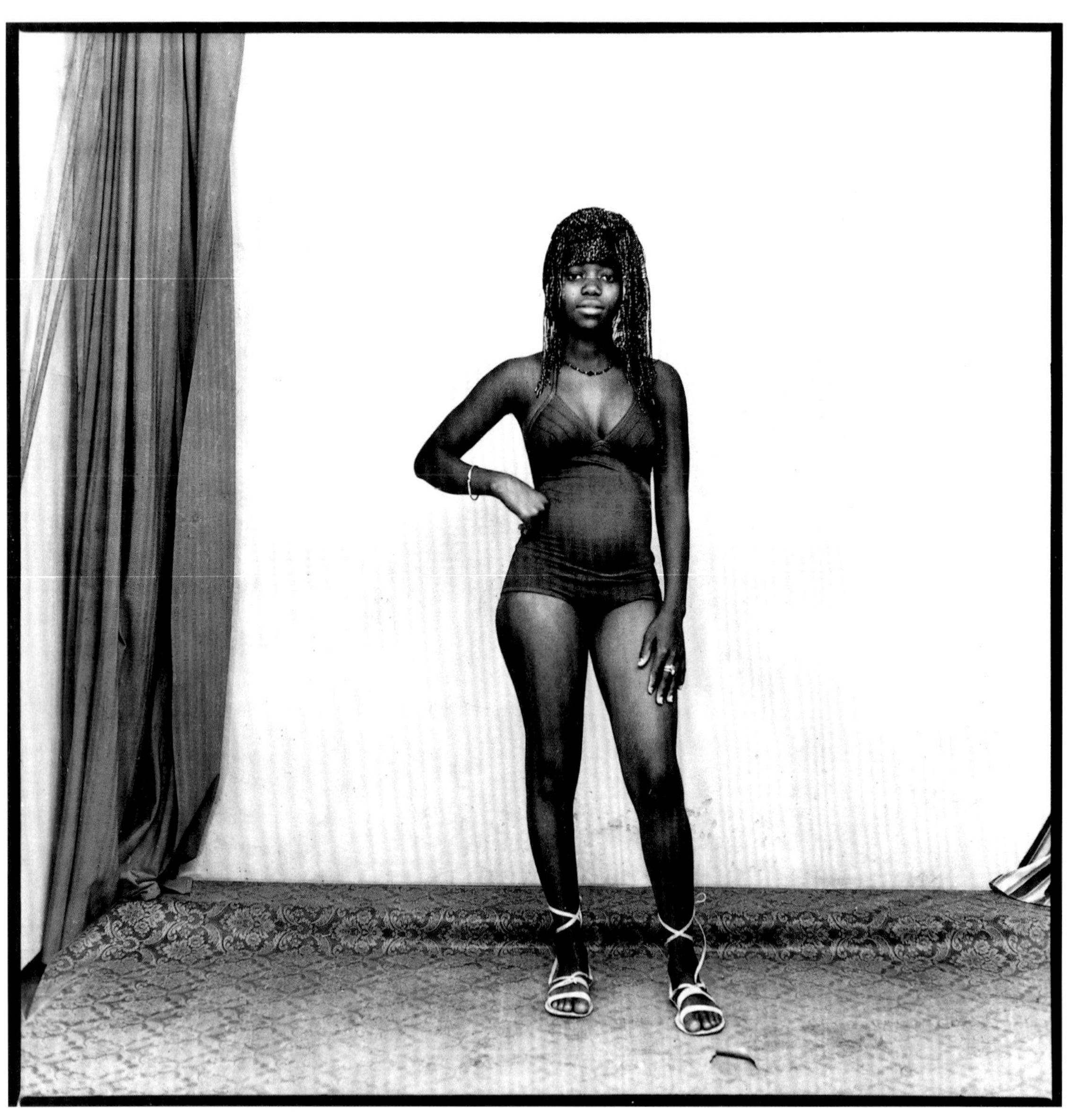

72 Malick Sidibé, *Mon maillot de bain* [My bathing suit], 1969

Checklist of the Exhibition

1
François-Edmond Fortier, Dakar, Senegal
1136. Afrique Occidentale, Jeunes Filles Ouolof [West Africa, Young Wolof Girls], c. 1900–10
Postcard, 8.9 x 13.9 cm
The Metropolitan Museum of Art, New York
Department of the Arts of Africa, Oceania, and the Americas
The Photograph Study Collection

2
Lisk-Carew Brothers, Freetown, Sierra Leone
Bundoo Girls, Sierra Leone, c. 1910
Postcard, halftone, 13.9 x 8.9 cm
The Metropolitan Museum of Art, New York
Department of the Arts of Africa, Oceania, and the Americas
The Photograph Study Collection

3
Khalilou, Libreville, Gabon
6. Ogooué Lambaréné—Jeunes Filles [Ogooué Lambaréné—Young Girls], c. 1900–15
Postcard, 8.9 x 13.9 cm
The Metropolitan Museum of Art, New York
Department of the Arts of Africa, Oceania, and the Americas
The Photograph Study Collection

4
Photographer unknown
14. Guinée Française—Conakry—Type Soussons [sic] [French Guinea—Conakry —Soussons (*sic*) Type], c. 1900–15
Postcard, 13.9 x 8.9 cm
The Metropolitan Museum of Art, New York
Department of the Arts of Africa, Oceania, and the Americas
The Photograph Study Collection

5
Photographer unknown
Conakry—Famille Soussou [Conakry—Soussou Family], c. 1900–15
Postcard, 13.9 x 8.9 cm
The Metropolitan Museum of Art, New York
Department of the Arts of Africa, Oceania, and the Americas
The Photograph Study Collection

6
F. Arkhurst
No. 6 The Young Native Girl, c. 1900–15
Postcard, lithograph, 13.9 x 8.9 cm
The Metropolitan Museum of Art, New York
Department of the Arts of Africa, Oceania, and the Americas
The Photograph Study Collection

7
Photographer unknown, Kindu, Belgian Congo
Printed by Nels, Belgium; published by Ferraz, Frères
Kindu—Négresses modernisées [Kindu—Modernized black women], c. 1915
Postcard, collotype, 13.6 x 8.7 cm
Eliot Elisofon Photographic Archives
National Museum of African Art, Smithsonian Institution

8
Photographer unknown
5. A Nioro (Soudan). Femmes et Fils de marchand ouolofes [At Nioro (Sudan), Wives and Son of Wolof Merchant], c. 1900–15
Postcard, 13.9 x 8.9 cm
The Metropolitan Museum of Art, New York
Department of the Arts of Africa, Oceania, and the Americas
The Photograph Study Collection

9
Photographer unknown
Nana Kwabene Wiafe II, Omanhene of Ofinsu, Ashanti, Gold Coast, BWA, c. 1900–15
Postcard, gelatin silver print, 13.9 x 8.9 cm
The Metropolitan Museum of Art, New York
Department of the Arts of Africa, Oceania, and the Americas
The Photograph Study Collection

10
François-Edmond Fortier, Dakar, Senegal
Afrique Occidentale—Soudan, 1014. Jeunes Femmes Arabes de Tombouctou [Young Arab women from Timbuktu, Mali], c. 1905
Postcard, collotype, 8.8 x 13.9 cm
Eliot Elisofon Photographic Archives
National Museum of African Art, Smithsonian Institution

11
J. Benyoumoff (distributor)
Dakar, Type Sénégalais [Dakar, Senegalese Type], c. 1900–15
Postcard, 13.9 x 8.9 cm

The Metropolitan Museum of Art, New York
Department of the Arts of Africa, Oceania, and the Americas
The Photograph Study Collection

12
G. Lerat
35. A.O.F.—Hte. Volta, Jeunes Toucouleurs [Upper Volta, Young Toucouleurs], c. 1900–15
Postcard, 13.9 x 8.9 cm
The Metropolitan Museum of Art, New York
Department of the Arts of Africa, Oceania, and the Americas
The Photograph Study Collection

13
Photographer unknown, possibly Côte d'Ivoire
Untitled (exterior studio portrait), c. 1900–50
Gelatin silver print, 23.4 x 17. 1 cm
The Metropolitan Museum of Art, New York
Purchase, Ross Family Fund, 1999 (1999.184.4)

14
Photographer unknown, possibly Côte d'Ivoire
Untitled (exterior studio portrait), c. 1900–50
Gelatin silver print, 23.4 x 17. 1 cm
The Metropolitan Museum of Art, New York
Purchase, Ross Family Fund, 1998 (1998.351.3)

Nos. 15–72 are courtesy of the Contemporary African Art Collection—The Pigozzi Collection, Geneva.

15
Malick Sidibé
Untitled, 1962–c. 1980
Gelatin silver print, 12.5 x 9 cm

16
Malick Sidibé
Untitled, 1962–c. 1980
Gelatin silver print, 13.5 x 9 cm

17
Malick Sidibé
Untitled, 1962–c. 1980
Gelatin silver print, 12.5 x 8.5 cm

18
Malick Sidibé
Untitled, 1962–c. 1980
Gelatin silver print, 18 x 12 cm

19
Malick Sidibé
Untitled, 1962–c. 1980
Gelatin silver print, 12 x 8.5 cm

20
Malick Sidibé
Untitled, 1962–c. 1980
Gelatin silver print, 12.5 x 9.5 cm

21
Malick Sidibé
Untitled, 1962–c. 1980
Gelatin silver print, 12.5 x 8.5 cm

22
Malick Sidibé
Untitled, 1962–c. 1980
Gelatin silver print, 12.5 x 8.5 cm

23
Malick Sidibé
Untitled, 1962–c. 1980
Gelatin silver print, 14 x 9 cm

24
Malick Sidibé
Untitled, 1962–c. 1980
Gelatin silver print, 12.5 x 8.5 cm

25
Malick Sidibé
Untitled, 1962–c. 1980
Gelatin silver print, 12.5 x 8.5 cm

26
Malick Sidibé
Untitled, 1962–c. 1980
Gelatin silver print, 12.5 x 9 cm

27
Malick Sidibé
Untitled, 1962–c. 1980
Gelatin silver print, 12.5 x 9 cm

28
Malick Sidibé
Untitled, 1962–c. 1980
Gelatin silver print, 12.5 x 8.5 cm

29
Seydou Keïta
Untitled, 1952–55
Gelatin silver print, 77 x 60 cm

30
Seydou Keïta
Untitled, 1952–55
Gelatin silver print, 77 x 60 cm

31
Seydou Keïta
Untitled, 1952–55
Gelatin silver print, 77 x 60 cm

32
Seydou Keïta
Untitled, 1950
Gelatin silver print, 77 x 60 cm

33
Seydou Keïta
Untitled, 1956
Gelatin silver print, 77 x 60 cm

34
Malick Sidibé
Les deux amis [The two friends], 1975
Gelatin silver print, 53 x 42 cm

35
Malick Sidibé
Au studio Malick [At Studio Malick], 1969
Gelatin silver print, 53 x 42 cm

36
Malick Sidibé
Amis des espagnoles [Friends of the Spanish], 1968
Gelatin silver print, 53 x 42 cm

37
Malick Sidibé
Tauré avec un mouton [Tauré with a sheep], 1962
Gelatin silver print, 47 x 37 cm

38
Malick Sidibé
Photo de studio, un enfant amoureux des fleurs [Studio photo, a child in love with flowers], 1975
Gelatin silver print, 53 x 42 cm

39
Malick Sidibé
Studio musique traditionelle du Mali Balafon [Studio, traditional balaphon music of Mali], 1975
Gelatin silver print, 53 x 42 cm

40
Seydou Keïta
Untitled, 1959
Gelatin silver print, 77 x 60 cm

41
Malick Sidibé
Portrait [Portrait], 1969
Gelatin silver print, 42 x 35 cm

42
Seydou Keïta,
Untitled, 1949–51
Gelatin silver print, 77 x 60 cm

43
Malick Sidibé
Je voudrais bien voir ma jupe [I would like to see my skirt], 1963
Gelatin silver print, 53 x 42 cm

44
Seydou Keïta
Untitled, 1952–55
Gelatin silver print, 77 x 60 cm

45
Malick Sidibé
Prise de vue dans une famille Sarakolé à Mission Bamako [Shot of a Sarakolé family at Mission Bamako], 1962
Gelatin silver print, 53 x 42 cm

46
Seydou Keïta
Untitled, 1959
Gelatin silver print, 77 x 60 cm

47
Seydou Keïta
Untitled, 1952–55
Gelatin silver print, 77 x 60 cm

48
Seydou Keïta
Untitled, 1956
Gelatin silver print, 77 x 60 cm

49
Malick Sidibé
Toute la famille en moto [The whole family on a motorcycle], 1962
Gelatin silver print, 53 x 42 cm

50
Seydou Keïta,
Untitled, 1956–57
Gelatin silver print, 77 x 60 cm

51
Malick Sidibé
Le photographe photographié [The photographer photographed], 1971
Gelatin silver print, 53 x 42 cm

52
Malick Sidibé
Il a tué une hyène [He killed a hyena], 1986
Gelatin silver print, 42 x 35 cm

53
Seydou Keïta
Untitled, 1957
Gelatin silver print, 77 x 60 cm

54
Malick Sidibé
Les jeunes circoncis et leur maître [The newly circumcised

and their teacher], 1983
Gelatin silver print, 77 x 60 cm

55
Malick Sidibé
Boxeurs en démonstration
[Boxers giving a demonstration], 1965
Gelatin silver print, 42 x 35 cm

56
Malick Sidibé
Tailleur et son modèle [Tailor and his model], 1974
Gelatin silver print, 77 x 60 cm

57
Seydou Keïta
Untitled, 1959
Gelatin silver print, 77 x 60 cm

58
Malick Sidibé
Femme Peuhl du Niger [Peul woman from Niger], 1970
Gelatin silver print, 42 x 35 cm

59
Malick Sidibé
Portrait de Mlle Kanté Sira
[Portrait of Miss Kanté Sira], 1965
Gelatin silver print, 53 x 42 cm

60
Seydou Keïta
Untitled, 1952–55
Gelatin silver print, 77 x 60 cm

61
Seydou Keïta
Untitled, 1949–51
Gelatin silver print, 77 x 60 cm

62
Seydou Keïta
Untitled, 1952–55
Gelatin silver print, 77 x 60 cm

63
Malick Sidibé
Je suis bien comme ça! [I look good like this!], n.d.
Gelatin silver print, 53 x 42 cm

64
Malick Sidibé
Jeune homme pattes d'éléphant sacoche et montre [Young man with bell-bottoms, bag, and watch], 1977
Gelatin silver print, 53 x 42 cm

65
Malick Sidibé
Un tailleur gentleman surnommé Mabus [A gentleman tailor by the name of Mabus], 1972
Gelatin silver print, 77 x 60 cm

66
Seydou Keïta
Untitled, 1956–57
Gelatin silver print, 77 x 60 cm

67
Malick Sidibé
Les jeunes bergers Peuhls
[Young Peul shepherds], 1972
Gelatin silver print, 53 x 42 cm

68
Seydou Keïta
Untitled, 1959
Gelatin silver print, 77 x 60 cm

69
Malick Sidibé, *Les trois amis avec motos, studio* [Three friends with motorbikes, studio], 1975
Gelatin silver print, 53 x 42 cm

70
Seydou Keïta,
Untitled, 1958
Gelatin silver print, 77 x 60 cm

71
Seydou Keïta
Untitled, 1952–55
Gelatin silver print, 77 x 60 cm

72
Malick Sidibé
Mon maillot de bain [My bathing suit], 1969
Gelatin silver print, 53 x 42 cm

73
Seydou Keïta
Magazine spread
"Sunday Best," *Harper's Bazaar* (May 1998)
Department of Photographs, Fogg Art Museum

74
Malick Sidibé
Magazine spread
"Avoir 33 ans à Bamako,"
Double, nouveau féminin
(February/March 2000)
Department of Photographs, Fogg Art Museum

Select Bibliography

Bigham, Elizabeth. "Issues of Authorship in the Portrait Photographs of Seydou Keïta." *African Arts* 32 (Spring 1999): 56–67, 94–96.

Chapuis, Frédérique, N'Goné Fall, and Pascal Martin Saint-Léon. *Anthology of African & Indian Ocean Photography*. Paris, 1999.

Cissé, Youssouf Tata. *Seydou Keïta*. Paris, 1995.

Diawara, Manthia. "Talk of the Town." *Artforum* 36 (February 1998): 64–71.

_____. "The 1960s in Bamako: Malick Sidibé and James Brown," The Andy Warhol Foundation for the Visual Arts, Paper Series on the Arts, Culture and Society, no. 11 (2001).

Enwezor, Okwui, Olu Oguibe, and Octavio Zaya. *In/sight: African Photographers, 1940 to the Present*. Exh. cat., Solomon R. Guggenheim Museum. New York, 1996.

French, Howard W. "Bamako Journal: Here, an Artist's Fame and Fortune Can Be Fatal." *New York Times*, 11 September 1997, A4.

Geary, Christraud M., and Virginia-Lee Webb, eds. *Delivering Views: Distant Cultures in Early Postcards*. Washington D.C., 1998.

Geary, Christraud M. *Seydou Keita, Photographer: Portraits From Bamako, Mali*. Exh. brochure, National Museum of African Art, Smithsonian Institution, Washington, D.C., 1996.

Herreman, Frank, and Roy Sieber, eds. *Hair in African Art and Culture*. New York, 2000.

Kerkham, Ruth. "Double Stitched: Colonial Pattern Making in the Works of Seydou Keïta and Yinka Shonibare." Paper presented at College Art Association annual meeting. Chicago, March 2001.

Loke, Margarett. "Inside Photography." *New York Times*, 11 July 1997, C23.

MacSweeney, Eve. "Sunday Best." *Harper's Bazaar* (May 1998): 172–79.

Magnin, André, ed. *Seydou Keïta*. Zurich/Berlin/New York, 1997.

_____. ed. *Malick Sidibé*. Zurich/Berlin/New York, 1998.

Malick Sidibé: Bamako 1962–1976. Exh. cat., Fondation Cartier pour l'Art Contemporain. Paris, 1995.

"Malick Sidibé with Lucas Michael." *Index Magazine* (May/June 1999): 24–31.

Mercer, Kobena. "Home from Home: Portraits from Places in Between." In *Self Evident*. Exh. cat., Ikon Gallery. Birmingham, England, 1995.

Nimis, Erika. *Photographes de Bamako de 1935 à nos jours*. Paris, 1998.

Pfeiffer, Kristine. *Malick Sidibé, Fotografie 1962–1976: Clubs und Twist und Chats Sauvages*. Stuttgart, 1997.

Porträt Afrika: Fotographische Positionen eines Jahrhunderts. Exh. cat., Haus der Kulturen der Welt. Berlin, 2000.

Prochaska, David. "Fantasia of the Photothèque: French Postcard Views of Colonial Senegal." *African Arts* 24 (October 1991): 40–47, 98.

Ravache, Martine. "Un photographe et son appareil: Seydou Keïta." *Photographies Magazine* 78 (July–August 1996): 66–67.

Seydou Keïta. Exh. cat., Fondation Cartier pour l'Art Contemporain. Paris, 1994.

Sidibé, Malick. "Avoir 33 ans à Bamako." *Double, nouveau féminin* 004 (February/March 2000): n.p.

Sprague, Steven F. "Yoruba Photography: How the Yoruba See Themselves." *African Arts* 12 (November 1978): 52–59, 107.

Storr, Robert. "Bamako: Full Dress Parade." *Parkett* 49 (May 1997): 24–34.

van der Plas, Els and Marlous Willemsen, eds. *The Art of African Fashion*. The Hague/Trenton, N. J./ Asmara, Eritrea, 1998.

Viditz-Ward, Vera. "Photography in Sierra Leone, 1850–1918." *Africa* 57 (1987): 510–17.

Villien-Rossi, M.-L. "Bamako, capitale du Mali." *Bulletin de l'Institut Fondamental d'Afrique Noire* 28, série B (1966): 249–380.

Wendl, Tobias, and Heike Behrend, eds. *Snap Me One!: Studiofotografen in Afrika*. Munich, 1998.

Wyman, James B., ed. "From the Background to the Foreground: The Photo Backdrop and Cultural Expression." Essays by Arjun Appadurai, Lucy R. Lippard, Avon Neal, and Sonia Iglesias y Cabrera and Maria del Carmen León. *Afterimage* 24 (March/ April 1997).